Gravity and Grace

Simone
Weil

Gravity and Grace

First complete English language edition

With an introduction and postscript by
Gustave Thibon

Translated by Emma Crawford and
Mario von der Ruhr

 London and New York

La Pesanteur et la grâce first published 1947
by Librairie PLON, Paris

First English edition published 1952
by Routledge & Kegan Paul

First published in Routledge Classics 2002
by Routledge
2 Park Square, Milton Park, Abingdon, Oxon, OX14 4RN
270 Madison Ave, New York NY 10016

Routledge is an imprint of the Taylor & Francis Group

Transferred to Digital Printing 2010

© 1947, 1999 Librairie PLON

Translation of Chapter entitled 'Israel' and Postscript ©2002
Mario von der Ruhr

Typeset in Joanna by RefineCatch Limited, Bungay, Suffolk

British Library Cataloguing in Publication Data
A catalogue record for this book is available from the British Library

Library of Congress Cataloging in Publication Data
A catalog record for this book has been requested

ISBN 0–415–29000–7 (hbk)
ISBN 0–415–29001–5 (pbk)

CONTENTS

INTRODUCTION

I find it hard to make public the extraordinary work of Simone Weil. Hitherto I have shared with only a few special friends the joy of knowing her personality and her mind, and now I have the painful impression of divulging a family secret. My one consolation lies in the certainty that through the inevitable profanation of publicity her testimony will reach other kindred souls.

I find it still harder to be obliged, in introducing this work, to speak incidentally of myself. *Secretum meum mihi*: the absence of reticence among many modern writers, the taste for autobiography and confession, the habit of admitting the public to the innermost recesses of an intimacy stripped of all reserve have never failed to surprise and scandalize me. Yet I owe it to myself—were it solely to justify the appearance of my name at the head of these papers—to explain the exceptional circumstances through which I came to know the real Simone Weil and to have the undeserved honour of presenting her thoughts to the world.

In June 1941 the Reverend Father Perrin, a Dominican friend

then living at Marseilles, sent me a letter which I do not happen to have kept but which ran more or less as follows: 'There is a young Jewish girl here, a graduate in philosophy and a militant supporter of the extreme left. She is excluded from the University by the new laws and is anxious to work for a while in the country as a farm hand. I feel that such an experiment needs supervision and I should be relieved if you could put her up in your house.' I had to think this letter over. Thank God I do not suffer from any *a priori* antisemitism, but what I know from experience of the qualities and faults of the Jewish temperament does not fit in any too well with my own and is particularly ill-adapted to the demands of everyday life together. There is an equally wide divergence between my instinctive reactions and those of a militant supporter of the extreme left. Moreover I am a little suspicious of graduates in philosophy, and as for intellectuals who want to return to the land, I am well enough acquainted with them to know that, with a few rare exceptions, they belong to that order of cranks whose undertakings generally come to a bad end. My first impulse was therefore to refuse. The wish to fall in with the suggestions of a friend, an unwillingness to spurn a soul which Destiny had placed in my path, the halo of sympathy surrounding the Jews as a result of the persecutions from which they were beginning to suffer, and, on the top of all this, a certain curiosity, made me change my mind.

A few days later Simone Weil arrived at my house. At first our relationship was friendly but uncomfortable. On the concrete plane we disagreed on practically everything. She went on arguing *ad infinitum* in an inexorably monotonous voice and I emerged from these endless discussions literally worn out. I enveloped myself in an armour of patience and courtesy in order to bear with her. Then, thanks to the privileges of a life which is shared, I gradually discovered that the side of her character which I found so impossible, far from revealing her real deep nature,

showed only her exterior and social self. In her case the respective positions of being and appearing were reversed: unlike most
people she gained immeasurably in an atmosphere of close
intimacy; with alarming spontaneity she displayed all that was
most unpleasing in her nature, but it needed much time and
affection, and a great deal of reserve had to be overcome, before
she showed what was best in her. She was just then beginning to
open with all her soul to Christianity, a limpid mysticism eman-
ated from her; in no other human being have I come across such
familiarity with religious mysteries; never have I felt the word
supernatural to be more charged with reality than when in contact
with her.

Such mysticism had nothing in common with those religious
speculations divorced from any personal commitment which are
all too frequently the only testimony of intellectuals who apply
themselves to the things of God. She actually experienced in its
heart-breaking reality the distance between 'knowing' and
'knowing with all one's soul', and the one object of her life was
to abolish that distance. I have witnessed too much of the daily
unfolding of her existence to be left with the slightest doubt as
to the authenticity of her spiritual vocation: her faith and
detachment were expressed in all her actions, sometimes with a
disconcerting disregard for the practical but always with absolute generosity. Her asceticism might seem exaggerated in our
century of half-measures where, to use the words of Léon Bloy,
'Christians gallop with due moderation to martyrdom' (and,
indeed, how great a scandal would be caused today by the eccentric practices of certain medieval saints?); nevertheless, it was
free from any emotional excess and it was impossible to discern
any change of level between her mortification and her inner life.
Finding my house too comfortable, she decided to live in an old
half-ruined farm belonging to my wife's parents and situated on
the banks of the Rhône. Every day she came to work and, when
she deigned to eat, she had her meals with us. Though delicate

and ill (she had suffered all her life from intolerable headaches, and an attack of pleurisy some years before she came to us had left its mark upon her) she worked on the land with tireless energy and often contented herself with blackberries from the wayside bushes for a meal. Every month she sent half her ration coupons to the political prisoners. As for her spiritual gifts, she distributed them with even more lavish generosity. Every evening after work she used to explain the great writings of Plato to me (I have never had time to learn Greek thoroughly). She did this with such educative genius that her teaching was as living as an original creation. Moreover she would put the same enthusiasm and love into teaching the rudiments of arithmetic to this or that backward urchin from the village. Her thirst to cultivate minds even led to some amusing misunderstandings. A kind of high-level equalitarianism led her to measure the capabilities of others by her own. There was scarcely anyone whom she did not consider able to receive the highest teaching. I remember a young working-class Lorraine girl in whom she thought she had detected signs of an intellectual vocation and to whom she poured forth at great length magnificent commentaries on the Upanishads. The poor child nearly died with boredom, but shyness and good manners prevented her from saying anything. . . .

In intimacy she was a charming and lively companion; she knew how to joke without bad taste and could be ironical without unkindness. Her extraordinary learning, so deeply assimilated that it could hardly be distinguished from the expression of her inner life, gave her conversation an unforgettable charm. She had a serious fault, however (or a rare quality according to the plane on which we place ourselves): it was to refuse to make any concession whatever to the requirements and conventions of social life. She always used to say everything she thought to everybody and in all circumstances. This sincerity, which was due chiefly to her deep respect for souls, caused her many misadventures. They were amusing for the most part, but some of them nearly resulted in tragedy at a time when it was not advisable to publish every truth from the housetops.

There is no question here of assessing the historical sources of her thought and the influences which may have affected her. Apart from the Gospel which was her daily spiritual food, she had a deep veneration for the great Hindu and Taoistic writings, for Homer, the Greek tragedies and above all for Plato, whom she interpreted in a fundamentally Christian manner. On the other hand she hated Aristotle, whom she regarded as the first to prepare a grave for the mystical tradition. Saint John of the Cross in the religious order, and Shakespeare, certain English mystical poets and Racine in the literary one, also left their mark on her mind. Among her contemporaries I can only think of Paul Valéry, and of Koestler in the *Spanish Testament*, of which she spoke to me with unmixed praise. Both her preferences and her dislikes were abrupt and final. She firmly believed that creation of real genius required a high level of spirituality and that it was impossible to attain to perfect expression without having passed through severe inner purgation. This insistence upon inner purity and authenticity made her pitiless for all the authors in whom she thought she could detect the slightest affectation, the slightest hint of insincerity or self-importance—Corneille, Hugo or Nietzsche for instance. For her the only thing that counted was a style stripped bare of all adornment, the perfect expression of the naked truth of the soul. 'The effort of expression', she wrote to me, 'has a bearing not only on the form but on the thought and on the whole inner being. So long as bare simplicity of expression is not attained, the thought has not touched or even come near to true greatness. . . . The real way of writing is to write as we translate. When we translate a text written in some foreign language, we do not seek to add anything to it; on the contrary, we are scrupulously careful not to add anything to it. That is how we have to try to translate a text which is not written down.'

After having passed some weeks with me, finding that she was treated with too much consideration, she decided to go and work in another farm so that, a stranger among strangers, she might share the lot of real agricultural labourers. I arranged for her to be taken on in the team of grape-gatherers of a large landowner in a neighbouring village. She worked there for more than a month with heroic regularity, always refusing, in spite of the fact that she was delicate and unaccustomed to the task, to spend shorter hours at it than the sturdy peasants who surrounded her. Her headaches were so bad that at times she had the impression of living through a nightmare. 'One day', she owned to me, 'I wondered if I had not died and fallen into hell without noticing, and whether hell did not consist of working eternally in a vineyard. . . .'

After this experience she went back to Marseilles, where her parents, who had been driven from Paris by the invasion, were living provisionally. I went sometimes to see her there in her little flat with its view stretching endlessly across the magnificent spaces of the sea. Meantime her parents were preparing to leave for the United States. Her devotion to her country in misfortune and her eagerness to share the fate of her persecuted friends made her hesitate for a long time about going with them. She eventually decided to do so in the hopes of being able to pass from there into Russia or England. I saw her for the last time at the beginning of 1942. At the station she gave me a portfolio crammed with papers, asking me to read them and to take care of them during her exile. As I parted from her I said jokingly, in an attempt to hide my feelings: 'Goodbye till we meet again in this world or the next!' She suddenly became serious and replied: 'In the next there will be no meeting again.' She meant that the limits which form our 'empirical self' will be done away with in the unity of eternal life. I watched her for a moment as she was disappearing down the street. We were not to meet again: contacts with the eternal in the time order are fearfully ephemeral.

On reaching home I went through Simone Weil's manuscripts. There were a dozen thick exercise books in which day by
day she recorded her thoughts. They ware interspersed with
quotations in all languages and with strictly personal notes. Until
then I had not read anything by her except a few poems and the
studies on Homer which appeared in the *Cahiers du Sud* under the
anagrammatical name of Emile Novis. All the writings which
are to be read farther on are drawn from these notebooks. I had
time to write once more to Simone Weil to let her know how
deeply I had been moved by what I read. From Oran she sent me
the following letter which, in spite of its personal character, I
have ventured to quote in full since it explains and justifies the
publication of this book:

'Dear Friend,

It seems as though the time has now really come for us to
say goodbye to each other. It will not be easy for me to hear from
you frequently. I hope that Destiny will spare the house at Saint
Marcel—the house inhabited by three beings who love each
other. That is someting very precious. Human existence is so
fragile a thing and exposed to such dangers that I cannot love
without trembling. I have never yet been able to resign myself to
the fact that all human beings except myself are not completely
preserved from every possibility of harm. That shows a serious
falling short in the duty of submission to God's will.

'You tell me that in my notebooks you have found, besides
things which you yourself had thought, others you had not
thought but for which you were waiting; so now they belong to
you, and I hope that after having been transmuted within you
they will one day come out in one of your works. For it is
certainly far better for an idea to be associated with your fortunes than with mine. I have a feeling that my own fortunes will
never be good in this world (it is not that I count on their being
better elsewhere; I cannot think that will be so). I am not a

person with whom it is advisable to link one's fate. Human beings have always more or less sensed this; but, I do not know for what mysterious reason, ideas seem to have less discernment. I wish nothing better for those which have come in my direction than that they should have a good establishment, and I should be very happy for them to find a lodging beneath your pen, whilst changing their form so as to reflect your likeness. That would somewhat diminish my sense of responsibility and the crushing weight of the thought that through my many defects I am incapable of serving the truth as I see it when in an inconceivable excess of mercy it seems to me that it deigns to allow me to behold it. I believe that you will take all that as simply as I say it to you. In the operation of writing, the hand which holds the pen, and the body and soul which are attached to it, with all their social environment, are things of infinitesimal importance for those who love the truth. They are infinitely small in the order of nothingness. That at any rate is the measure of importance I attach in this operation not only to my own personality but to yours and to that of any other writer I respect. Only the personality of those whom I more or less despise matters to me in such a domain. . . .

'I do not know whether I have already said it to you, but as to my notebooks, you can read whatever passages you like from them to whomever you like, but you must leave none of them in the hands of anyone else. . . . If you hear nothing of me for three or four years, you can consider that you have complete ownership of them.

'I am saying all this to you so that I can go away with a freer mind. I only regret not being able to confide to you all that I still bear undeveloped within me. Luckily, however, what is within me is either valueless or else it exists outside me in a perfect form, in a place of purity where no harm can come to it and whence it will always be able to come down again. That being so, nothing concerning me can have any kind of importance.

'I also like to think that after the slight shock of separation you will not feel any sorrow about whatever may be in store for me, and that if you should sometimes happen to think of me you will do so as one thinks of a book one read in childhood. I do not want ever to occupy a different place from that in the hearts of those I love, because then I can be sure of never causing them any unhappiness.

'I shall never forget the generosity which made you say and write to me some of those things which warm and cheer us even when, as in my case, it is impossible to believe them. They are a support all the same—perhaps too much so. I do not know whether we shall be able to go on corresponding much longer. We must however think of that as unimportant. . . .'

If I had been a saint I should have been able to accept the offer which this letter contained. I should also have been able to accept it if I had been an utterly despicable individual. In the first case my *self* would not have counted at all, and in the second it would have been the only thing that did count. As I am neither the one nor the other the question did not arise.

Simone Weil wrote to me again from Casablanca, then a last time from New York. After that the occupation of the free zone by the Germans held up our correspondence. In November 1944, when I was expecting her return to France, I heard from friends we had in common that she had died a year before in London.

Simone Weil was too pure to have many secrets; she spoke of herself as simply as of everything else. It would be quite easy for me by referring to my memories and to our conversations together to give a very good portrait of her from the superficial point of view, a portrait of which the originality would delight all those who love anecdotes and details from actual experience. The affection I bore her makes that impossible. A brother cannot speak about his sister as one writer of another. Moreover, to season such highly spiritual fare with pictorial condiments would result in somewhat bad taste. I will therefore confine myself to outlining the main features of her life before and after our meeting.

She was born in Paris in 1909 and after having been one of Alain's pupils entered the Ecole Normale Supérieure very young, there to do brilliantly in her *agrégation*,[1] her subject being philosophy. After that she taught in a number of secondary schools and very soon began to take part in politics. It goes without saying that the revolutionary convictions, which she aired with complete disregard for professional or social conventions, brought her into difficulties with the authorities. She rose above such difficulties with calm disdain. To an inspector who threatened her with reports which might have led to her dismissal she smilingly replied 'I have always considered dismissal as the normal crowning of my career.' She fought in the ranks of the extreme left, but she never joined any political body, contenting herself with defending the weak and oppressed irrespective of party or race. Wishing to share to the uttermost the lot of the poor, she asked for a holiday and took a job in the Renault works, where, without letting anyone know who she was, she worked for a year on the benches. She hired a room in the workmen's district and lived entirely on her meagre earnings. An attack of pleurisy put an end to this experiment. At the time of the Spanish War she entered the ranks of the Reds, but she made a point of never using her weapons and was more an animator than a fighter. A physical accident (she inadvertently scalded her feet) necessitated her being brought back to France. In these tragic circumstances, as throughout her life, her parents, to whom she was deeply attached but whom she kept in an agony

---

[1] Competitive examination conducted by the State for admission to posts on the teaching staff of *lycées*.

of anxiety by her heroic extravagances, surrounded her with constant care, which certainly put off the inevitable outcome of an existence so free from anything tending to keep it captive in the flesh. 'The strength which the Karamazovs draw from the lowest part of their nature' and which keeps man glued to this earth was strangely lacking in her. . . .

Before recalling Simone Weil's attitude during the developments which caused the French to be so deeply divided during the years 1940 to 1944, I want to stress the fact that it would be harmful to her memory were the eternal and transcendent part of her message to be interpreted in the light of present-day politics and confused with party quarrels. No faction, no social ideology has the right to claim her. Her love of the people and her hatred of all oppression are not enough to place her among the leftists any more than her denial of progress and her cult for tradition authorize us to class her on the right. She put the same passionate enthusiasm into her political activities as into everything else, but far from making an idol of an idea, a nation or a class, she knew that the social field is above all the abode of what is relative and evil ('to contemplate the social scene', she wrote, 'is as effective a purification as to withdraw from the world, and that is why I have not been wrong in mixing for so long a time in politics'). She knew that in these matters the duty of a supernatural soul does not consist in fanatically embracing a party but in ceaselessly trying to restore the balance by taking the side of the defeated and the oppressed. It was thus that, in spite of her dislike for Communism, she wanted to go to Russia when that country was bleeding under the heel of the Germans. This idea of *counterbalancing* is essential in her conception of political and social activity: 'If we know in what direction the scales of society are tilted we must do what we can to add weight to the lighter side. Although the weight may be something evil, if we handle it with this motive we shall perhaps not be tainted by it. But we must have a conception of equal balance and be always ready to change sides like Justice—that fugitive from the camp of conquerors.'

At the time of the Armistice this state of mind inclined her towards the movement of divers origins and ends which is now referred to under the global term of Resistance. Before she left for America she had had a bone to pick with the police of the French State and there is no doubt as to what would have been her fate if she had still been in France at the time of the great Gestapo raids. As soon as she reached the United States she took steps to become enrolled in the forces of the Resistance. She left for London in 1942 and worked there for some time under M. Maurice Schumann. She begged persistently to be sent on a mission to France, but her racial type was too recognizable to allow of this. Being unable to expose herself to the dangers which then hung over the lives of the French, she wanted at least to share their privations and strictly kept to rations which never exceeded the amount allocated by food coupons in France. This diet soon got the better of her health which, even to start with, was variable. Worn out with hunger and phthisis, she had to go into hospital. There she suffered acutely on account of any special comforts which were ordered for her. I had already noticed this characteristic when she was at my home: she had a horror of being given privileges and fiercely shook herself free from any watchful care which aimed at raising her above the common level. She only felt at ease on the lowest rung of the social ladder, lost among the masses of poor folk and outcasts of this world. She was moved to the country and died there after having shown her joy at once more seeing Nature. I have no details of her end. 'The death agony', she once said, 'is the supreme dark night which is necessary even for the perfect if they are to attain to absolute purity, and for that reason it is better that it should be bitter.' I dare to think that her life had been hard enough for her to have been granted a peaceful passage.

Simone Weil's writings belong to the category of very great work which can only be weakened and spoilt by a commentary. My sole reason for introducing these texts is that my friendship with the author and the long conversations we had together clear away my difficulties in entering into her thought and make it easier for me to replace in their exact setting and their organic context certain formulae which are too bald or need to be elaborated. We must, in fact, remember that we are here concerned, as in Pascal's case, with simple waiting stones set out day by day, often hurriedly, with a view to a more complete building which, alas! never came into being.

The texts are bare and simple[1] like the inner experience which they express. No padding is interposed between the life and the word; soul, thought and expression form one block with no joins in it. Even if I had not known Simone Weil personally, her style alone would in my opinion guarantee the authenticity of her testimony. What is most striking in these thoughts is the comprehensiveness of their possible applications; their simplicity simplifies everything they touch; they transport us to those summits of being from which the eye embraces in one glance an infinity of horizons one above the other. 'We must welcome all opinions,' she used to say, 'but they must be arranged vertically and kept on suitable levels.' Again: 'Whatever is real enough to allow of superposed interpretations is innocent and good.' This sign of greatness and purity is found on every page of her work.

Here for instance is a thought which wipes out the ancient quarrel between optimism and pessimism—that quarrel which Leibniz could not settle: 'There is every degree of distance between the creature and God. A distance in which the love of God is impossible: matter, plants, animals. Evil is so complete

---

[1] This is the explanation of certain repetitions and negligences of style which we have scrupulously respected throughout.

there that it destroys itself: there is no longer any evil: mirror of divine innocence. We are at the point where love is just possible. It is a great privilege since the love which unites is in proportion to the distance. God has created a world which is not the best possible but which contains the whole range of good and evil. We are at the point where it is as bad as possible because beyond is the stage where evil becomes innocence.'

Or there is this other thought which throws light on the problem of evil and reaches to the very secrets of divine love: 'All created things refuse to satisfy me as ends. Such is the extreme mercy of God towards me. And that very thing constitutes evil. Evil is the form which the mercy of God takes in this world.' And then there is this abrupt and final refutation of all such philosophers as Schopenhauer or Sartre who argue that the presence of evil in the world justifies a fundamental pessimism: 'To say that the world is not worth anything, that this life is of no value, and to give evil as the proof is absurd, for if these things are worthless what does evil take from us?'

Or again, we find the law of the insertion of the higher into the lower formulated thus: 'Every order which transcends another can only be introduced into it under the form of something infinitely small.' This completes and deepens the law of the three orders of Pascal. The world of life does indeed appear to be infinitely small in the midst of the material world: what do living beings represent when compared to the huge mass of the planet and perhaps of the cosmos? It is the same with the spiritual world in relation to the world of life: there are at least 500,000 living species on the earth, of which only one possesses 'il ben dell' intelletto'. And as for the world of grace, it, in turn, appears infinitely small against the mass of our secular thoughts and affections: the gospel illustrations of the leaven and the grain of mustard seed are clear enough evidence of this 'characteristic of being infinitesimal which belongs to pure goodness'.

Impregnating the whole of Simone Weil's work is the driving

force of an intense desire for inward purification which comes out even in her metaphysics and her theology. Stretching out with all her soul towards a pure and absolute goodness of which nothing here below provides her with a proof but which she feels to be more real than anything existing in and around her, she seeks to establish her faith in this perfect being upon a base which no stroke of fortune, no affliction, no surging wave either of mind or matter can shake. For that, it is important before all things to eliminate from the inner life all forms of illusion and compensation (imaginative piety, the 'consolations' of religion, a crude faith in the immortality of the self, etc.) which too often usurp the name of God and which are really no more than shelters for our weakness or our pride: 'We have to be careful about the level on which we place the infinite. If we put it on the level which is only suitable for the finite it does not much matter what name we give it.'

Creation reflects God by its beauty and harmony, but, through the evil and death which abide in it and the blind necessity by which it is governed, it also reflects the absence of God. We have issued from God: that means that we bear his imprint and it means also that we are separated from him. The etymology of the word to exist (to be placed outside) is very illuminating in this respect: we can say we exist, we cannot say we are. God who is Being has in a sense effaced himself so that we can exist: he has given up being everything in order that we might exist; he has dispossessed himself in our favour of his own necessity, which is identical with goodness, to allow another necessity to reign which is alien and indifferent to good. The central law of this world, from which God has withdrawn by his very act of creation, is the law of gravity, which is to be found analogously in every stage of existence. Gravity is the force which above all others draws us from God. It impels each creature to seek everything which can preserve or enlarge it and, as Thucydides says, to exercise all the power of which it is capable. Psychologically it is shown by all those motives which are directed towards asserting or reinstating the self, by all those secret subterfuges (lies of the inner life, escape in dreams or false ideals, imaginary encroachments on the past and the future, etc.) which we make use of to bolster up from inside our tottering existence, that is to say, to remain apart from and opposed to God.

Simone Weil presents the problem of evil as follows: 'How can we escape from that which corresponds to gravity in ourselves?' By grace alone. In order to come to us God passes through the infinite thickness of time and space; his grace changes nothing in the play of those blind forces of necessity and chance which guide the world; it penetrates into our souls as a drop of water makes its way through geological strata without affecting their structure, and there it waits in silence until we consent to become God again. Whereas gravity is the work of creation, the work of grace consists of 'decreating' us. God consented through love to cease to be everything so that we might be something; we must consent through love to cease to be anything so that God may become everything again. It is therefore a question of abolishing the self within us, 'that shadow thrown by sin and error which stops the light of God and which we take for a being.' Without this utter humility, this unconditional consent to be nothing, all forms of heroism and immolation are still subject to the law of gravity and falsehood: 'We can offer nothing short of ourselves. Otherwise what we term our offering is merely a label attached to a compensatory assertion of the "I"'.

In order to kill the self we must be ready to endure all the wounds of life, exposing ourselves naked and defenceless to its fangs, we must accept emptiness, an unequal balance, we must never seek compensations and, above all, we must suspend the work of our imagination, 'which perpetually tends to stop up the cracks through which grace flows.' Every sin is an attempt to fly from emptiness. We must also renounce the past and future, for the self is nothing but a coagulation of past and future around a present which is always falling away. Memory and hope destroy the wholesome effect of affliction by providing an unlimited field where we can be lifted up in imagination ('I used to be', 'I shall be' . . .), but faithfulness to the passing moment reduces man truly to nothing and thus opens to him the gates of eternity.

The self should be destroyed in us from within by love. But its destruction can also be brought about from without by extreme suffering and degradation. There are vagrants and prostitutes who have no more self-esteem than the saints and whose life is confined to the passing moment. Therein lies the tragedy of degradation. It is irreparable, not because the self which it destroys is precious, for the self is made to be destroyed, but because it prevents God from effecting the destruction himself and robs eternalizing love of its prey.

Simone Weil makes a sharp distinction between this supernatural immolation and all forms of human grandeur and heroism. Here below God is the feeblest and most destitute of beings; his love, unlike that of idols, does not fill the carnal part of the soul; to go to him we have to labour in the void, to refuse every intoxication of passion or pride which veils the horrible mystery of death, and to allow ourselves to be guided only by the 'still, small voice' spoken of in the Bible—a voice inaudible to the senses and unnoticed by the self. 'To say to Christ as Saint Peter did: "I will always be faithful to thee", is to deny him already, for it is to suppose that the source of fidelity is in ourselves and not in grace. As he was chosen, this denial was made known to all men and to himself. How many others boast in the same way—and never understand.' It is easy to die for something forceful because participation in force produces an intoxication which stupefies us. But it is supernatural to die for something weak: thousands of men were able to die heroically for Napoleon, whilst Christ in his agony was deserted by his disciples (the sacrifice was easier later on for the martyrs, for they were already upheld by the social force of the Church). 'Supernatural love has no contact with force, moreover it does not protect the soul against the coldness of force, the coldness of steel. Only an earthly attachment, if it has in it enough energy, can afford protection against the coldness of steel. Armour is made of metal in the same way as the sword. If we want a love which will protect the soul from wounds we must love something other than God.'

The hero wears armour, the saint is naked. Now armour, while keeping off blows, prevents any direct contact with reality and above all makes it impossible to enter the third dimension which is that of supernatural love. If things are really to exist for us they have to penetrate within us. Hence the necessity for being naked: nothing can enter into us while armour protects us both from wounds and from the depths which they open up. All sin is an attack against the third dimension, an attempt to bring back to the plane of unreality and painlessness an emotion which seeks to penetrate to the depths. This law is inexorable: we lessen our own suffering to the extent that we weaken our inner and direct communion with reality. At the extreme limit of this process life is entirely stretched out on the surface: we suffer no more except in a dream, for existence, reduced to two dimensions, becomes flat like a dream. This holds good for consolations, illusions, boasting and all the compensatory reactions by which we try to fill up the hollows bitten into us by reality. Every empty place or hollow does in fact imply the presence of the third dimension; it is not possible to enter into a surface, and to fill up a hole is equivalent to taking refuge in isolation on the surface. The adage of ancient physics: 'Nature abhors a vacuum', is strictly true in psychology. But this vacuum is precisely what grace needs in order to come into us.

This process of 'decreation', which is the only way of salvation, is the work of grace and not of the will. Man does not pull himself up to heaven by the hair. The will is only useful for servile tasks; it controls the right use of natural virtues, which are pre-requisites of the work of grace, in the same way as the ploughman's effort must precede the sowing. But the divine seed comes from elsewhere. . . . In this realm Simone Weil, like Plato and Malebranche, considers attention to be of far more importance than will: 'We must be indifferent to good and evil, *really* indifferent; that is to say, we must turn the light of attention equally on each of them. Then the good will triumph by an automatic phenomenon.' It is precisely this superior automatism which has to be created; it is not obtained by tightening up the *self* and 'going beyond one's capacity' (*forçant son talent*) for doing good (nothing is more degrading than a noble action performed in an unworthy spirit) but by arriving through self-effacement and love at that state of perfect docility to grace whence goodness spontaneously emanates. 'Action is the pointer which shows the balance. We must not touch the pointer but the weight.' Unfortunately it is easier to tamper with the pointer than to alter our own weight in these 'golden scales of Zeus'.

So, then, religious attention raises us above the 'aberration of opposites' and the choice between good and evil—'Choice, a notion belonging to a low level'. So long as I hesitate between doing or not doing a bad action (for instance, possessing or not such and such a woman who offers herself to me, betraying or not betraying some friend), even if I choose the good I scarcely rise above the evil I reject. In order for my 'good' action to be really pure, I must dominate this miserable oscillation so that the righteousness of my outward behaviour is the exact expression of my inward necessity. Holiness is like degradation in this respect[1]; just as an utterly despicable man does not hesitate to

---

[1] This is the postulate of Hermes: the highest resembles the lowest—a central law of being of which Simone Weil gives endless illustrations in her work. Thus the non-resistance of the saints is outwardly indistinguishable from cowardice; supreme wisdom ends in a sense of ignorance, the motions of grace have the

possess himself of a woman if his passion demands it or to betray a friend if it is in his interest to do so, a saint has no choice to make about remaining pure and faithful: he cannot do anything else; he goes towards goodness like the bee towards a flower. Goodness which we choose by balancing it against evil has scarcely anything but social value; to the eyes of Him 'who seeth in secret' it proceeds from the same motives and is marked by the same vulgarity as evil. Hence the kinship often observed between certain forms of 'virtue' and the corresponding sin: theft and the bourgeois respect for property, adultery and a 'respectable woman', the savings-bank and waste, etc. Real goodness is not opposed to evil (in order to oppose something directly it is necessary to be on the same level); it transcends and effaces it. 'What evil violates is not goodness, for goodness is inviolate; only a degraded good can be violated.'

The soul engaged in the pursuit of pure goodness comes up against irreducible contradictions. Contradiction is the criterion of reality. 'Our life is impossibility, absurdity. Everything that we want is in contradiction with the conditions or consequences which are attached to it. It is because we ourselves are a contradiction, being creatures, being God and infinitely other than God.' Have countless children, for instance, and you are bringing about overpopulation and war (Japan is a typical case of this); improve the material conditions of a nation and you are in danger of impairing its soul; devote yourself entirely to someone and you will cease to exist for him, etc. Only imaginary good things have no contradiction in them: the girl who wants to have numerous offspring, the social reformer who dreams of the people's well-being, etc., meet with no obstacles so long as they do not pass on to action; they sail gaily forward in a sea of pure but fictitious goodness; the shock of hitting the rocks is the

inevitability of animal instincts. ('I have become as a beast of burden before thy face' . . .), detachment is like indifference, etc.

signal which wakens them. We must accept this contradiction—
the sign of our misery and our greatness—in all its bitterness. It
is through fully experiencing and suffering from the absurdity as
such of this universe where good and evil are mixed that we
attain to the pure goodness whose kingdom is not of this world.
'That action is pure which we can accomplish by keeping our
intention totally directed towards pure and impossible goodness, without disguising from ourselves by any lie either the
attraction or the impossibility of pure goodness.' Instead of
filling the space which stretches between necessity and goodness with dreams (faith in God as a temporal father, science,
progress . . .) we must receive the two branches of contradiction
just as they are and allow ourselves to be torn asunder by their
distance. And it is in this tearing, which is as it were a reflection
in man of the creative act which rends God, that we rediscover
the original identity of necessity and goodness: 'This world, in
so far as it is quite empty of God, is God himself. Necessity, in so
far as it is absolutely distinct from goodness, is goodness itself.
That is why all consolation in affliction separates us from love
and from truth. Therein lies the mystery of mysteries. When we
touch it we are secure.' He, therefore, who refuses to accept
confusion is marked for suffering. From Antigone whom the
guardian of the temporal city called upon to go and love among
the shades, down to Simone Weil herself whom human injustice
crucified until she was in her grave, affliction is the lot of all
those lovers of the absolute who are astray in this world of
relative things: 'If we want only goodness we are opposed to the
law which links good to evil as the illuminated object to the
shadow, and, being opposed to the universal law of the world, it
is inevitable that we should fall into affliction.' In so far as the
soul is not completely emptied of itself, this thirst for pure
goodness leads to the suffering of expiation; in a perfectly innocent soul it produces redemptive suffering: 'To be innocent is to
bear the weight of the whole universe. It is to throw in the

counterweight to restore the balance.' Thus purity does not abolish suffering; on the contrary it deepens it to infinity whilst giving it an eternal meaning: 'The extreme greatness of Christianity lies in the fact that it does not seek a supernatural cure for suffering, but a supernatural use of it.'

This mystery of suffering which 'decreates' man and gives him back to God finds its centre in the mystery of the Incarnation. If God had not been incarnate, man who suffers and dies would have become in a sense greater than God. But God made himself man and died on the Cross. 'God abandoned God. God emptied himself: these words enfold the meaning both of the Creation and of the Incarnation with the Passion. . . . To teach us that we are nothing (non-être) God made himself nothing.' In other words God became a creature in order to teach us how to undo the creature in ourselves, and the act of love by which he was separated from himself brings us back to him. Simone Weil sees the essence of the mediatorial function of Jesus Christ in his assumption of the human condition with all that is most miserable and tragic in it: the signs and miracles constitute the human and relatively low part of his mission; the supernatural part consists of the agony, the sweat of blood, the Cross and his vain calls to an unanswering heaven. The words of the Redeemer: 'My God, my God, why hast thou forsaken me?' which sum up all the agony of the creature thrown into the midst of time and evil and to which the Father replies only with silence—these words alone are enough proof for her of the divinity of Christianity.

Man only finds salvation by living in the bare instant, renouncing the past and future. That rules out the modern myth of the indefinite progress of humanity, even when it is presented under the form of a divine education. There are few ideas which are as impious as this one, for it tends to make us seek in the future what eternity alone can give, that is to say, to turn away from God. 'Nothing can have a destination which is not its origin. The contrary idea, the idea of progress—poison. The plant which bears such fruit should be torn up by the roots.' This does not mean to say that humanity cannot acquire anything in the course of time, but such progress, in so far as it is temporal, can never be indefinite, for duration always ends by devouring what it has brought to birth. Time, accepted as irremediably different from eternity, is for us the door opening onto the eternal: we must not make of it a substitute for eternity.

From this essential condition of salvation, the necessity of living in the pure instantaneous present and of toiling regardless of results, Simone Weil draws a magnificent spirituality of manual work. Such work puts man into direct contact with the inherent absurdity and contradiction of earthly life and thus, if the worker does not lie, it enables him to touch heaven. 'Work makes us experience in an exhausting manner the phenomenon of finality rebounding like a ball; to work in order to eat, to eat in order to work. . . . If we regard one of the two as an end, or the one and the other taken separately, we are lost. Only the cycle contains the truth.' But in order to compass this cycle we must turn from the future and rise up to the eternal. 'It is not religion but revolution which is the opium of the people.'

Here below, a thousand relative objects bearing the label of absolute come between the soul and God. So long as man does not consent to become nothing in order to be everything he needs idols. 'Idolatry is a vital necessity in the cave.' And among these idols the social one of the collective soul is the most powerful and dangerous. Most sins can be traced back to the social element. They spring from a thirst to appear and to dominate. It is not that Simone Weil rejects the social element as such; she knows that our environment, roots and traditions form bridges, metaxu between earth and heaven; what she repudiates is the totalitarian city—symbolized by the 'Great Beast' of Plato and the Beast of the Apocalypse—whose power and prestige usurp God's place in the soul. Whether it shows itself under a conservative or a revolutionary aspect, whether it consists of adoring the present or the future city, social idolatry always tends to stifle and to replace the true mystic tradition. All the persecutions of prophets and saints are due to it; through it Antigone and Joan of Arc were condemned and Jesus Christ crucified. The social Beast offers man a substitute for religion which allows him to transcend his individuality without surrendering his *self* and so, at small cost, to dispense with God; a social imitation of the highest virtues is possible by which they are immediately degraded into pharisaism: 'The pharisee is he who is virtuous out of obedience to the Great Beast.'

Two nations of antiquity illustrate this idolatry of the collective soul: Israel and Rome. 'Rome is the Great Beast of atheism and materialism, adoring nothing but itself. Israel is the Great Beast of religion. Neither the one nor the other is likable. The Great Beast is always repulsive.' The conflict between Israel and Rome, in which Nietzsche saw the duel of two irreconcilable conceptions of life, was reduced for Simone Weil to a struggle between two totalitarianisms of the same nature. It must however be emphasized that her antisemitism, which was so violent that the continuity established by the Church between the Old and New Testaments was one of the chief obstacles to her becoming a Catholic, was of a purely spiritual order and consequently had nothing in common with what goes by that name today. She had, for example, the same aversion for Hitlerian antisemitism as for the Jewish idea of a temporal Messianic rule. How many times did she not speak to me of the Jewish roots of antisemitism! She was fond of saying that Hitler hunted on the same ground as the Jews and only persecuted them in order to resuscitate under another name and to his own advantage their tribal god, terrestrial, cruel and exclusive. Her horror of the social idol was of course extended to all other forms of totalitarian mysticism and in particular to Marxism. Even the Catholic Church, which moreover she admired in many of its aspects, did not escape her criticism as a social body. Its Jewish and Roman sources, its connexion with temporal things, its organization and hierarchy, its councils, certain formulae such as 'no salvation outside the Church' or *anathema sit* and some of its historical records such as the Inquisition, etc., appeared to her to be forms (of a higher order, but nevertheless infinitely to be feared) of social idolatry. Yet she never ceased to believe in the divine presence and inspiration within the Church. 'Happily, the gates of hell will not prevail', she wrote towards the end of her life; 'there remains an incorruptible core of truth.'

Such are the main lines of Simone Weil's thought. The schematic nature of this exposition necessarily leaves on one side a thousand touches which give precision, strength and balance to her doctrine. But an introduction, as its name suggests, can be no more than an invitation to cross the threshold.

I may say that my friendship and veneration for Simone Weil, the pain of losing her and the joy of finding her again each day above and beyond death, the fact that I constantly feed upon her thought and, above all, the insuperable reserve with which all true intimacy is accompanied, combine to make the effort of detachment required of me in undertaking an objective and critical analysis of her work almost impossible.

I am a Catholic, Simone Weil was not. I have never doubted for a second that she was infinitely more advanced than I am in the experimental knowledge of supernatural truths, but outwardly she always remained on the borders of the Church and was never baptized. One of the last letters she wrote me shows very clearly her attitude with regard to Catholicism: 'At this moment I should be more ready to die for the Church, if one day before long it should need anyone to die for it, than I should be to enter it. To die does not commit one to anything, if one to say such a thing; it does not contain anything in the nature of a lie. . . . At present I have the impression that I am lying whatever I do, whether it be by remaining outside the Church or by entering it. The question is to know where there is less of a lie. . . .' As to whether Simone Weil were a heroic lover of Jesus Christ, my conviction has never changed; all the same her doctrine, though it is within the orbit of the great Christian truths, contains nothing specifically Catholic and she never accepted the universal authority of the Church. Now a Catholic who has to assess the thought of a non-Catholic has difficulty in avoiding two opposite extremes. The first consists of applying the principles of speculative theology to the thought in question and mercilessly condemning everything which, seen from outside, does not appear to be strictly orthodox. This method has the advantage of railings, which are always necessary on the bridges leading to God, but, used without understanding or love, it is in danger of degenerating into an abuse of the evangelical precept: 'if thine eye offend thee . . .'. For my part, as I am neither a theologian nor specially entrusted with the defence of the deposit of Christian faith, I do not feel myself in any way qualified for such an undertaking. The last thing I want to do is to set myself up as an official theologian who, armed with a sort of Baedeker of divine things, presumes to pronounce final judgment on the report, even incomplete, of a heroic explorer. . . . The second danger consists of trying at whatever cost to bend the thought one is studying into conformity with Catholic truth. That is a manifest abuse of the text 'compel them to come in'. We think that whatever is true or pure in a human life or work finds its place naturally in the Catholic synthesis without being forced or twisted in order to do so. We have no need to grasp everything for ourselves like a miser trying to increase his treasure, for everything already belongs to us who belong to Christ.

It is not for me to decide how far the ideas of Simone Weil are or are not orthodox. I will confine myself to showing—on purely personal evidence—how far a Christian can interpret these ideas in order to find nourishment for his spiritual life.

I shall be particularly careful not to pick a quarrel with

Simone Weil about words. Her vocabulary is that of the mystics and not of the speculative theologians: it does not seek to express the eternal order of being but the actual journey of the soul in search of God. This is the case with all spiritual writers. When in the *Dialogue* of Saint Catherine of Siena Christ says to her; 'I am that which is, thou art that which is not', this formula which reduces the creature to pure nothingness cannot be accepted on the plane of ontological knowledge. It is the same with the expressions used by so many mystics who speak of the poverty of God, of his dependence in relation to the creature, etc.: they are true in the order of love and false in the order of being. Jacques Maritain was the first to show, with perfect metaphysical precision, that these two vocabularies do not contradict each other, for one is related to speculative and the other to practical and affective knowledge.

Two things in particular in Simone Weil's work have shocked the few friends to whom I have shown her manuscripts. First the absolute division which she seems to establish between the created world and a transcendent God who has tied his own hands in the presence of evil and who abandons the universe to the sport of chance and absurdity: there is a danger lest this clean cut should lead to the elimination of the idea of Providence in history and of the notion of progress, and as a result to a misunderstanding of the values and duties of this present world. In the second place her fear of the social element is likely to lead to the isolation of the individual in a proud self-sufficiency.

I repeat that Simone Weil speaks as a mystic and not as a metaphysician. I am prepared to admit, and I do so readily, that the tendency of her genius which inclines her constantly to stress the irreducible nature of supernatural reality often leads her to overlook the meeting places and transitional stages between nature and grace. Nothing is more certain than that she has misunderstood certain aspects of Christian piety. But that does not authorize us to assert that the aspect she describes is not

Christian. No human experience—if we except that of Christ—has ever embraced supernatural truth in its totality. Saint John of the Cross, for instance, does not emphasize the same divine realities as Saint Bonaventura. There are several schools of spirituality, and, if we substitute the word 'God' for 'world', we can say of the mystics what the poet said of men in general:

'Dass jeder sieht die Welt in seinem Sinn
Und jeder siehet recht, so viel ist Sinn darin!'

If, as the Gospel says, there are many mansions in heaven, there are also many roads which lead to heaven.

Simone Weil chose the negative road: 'There are people for whom everything is salutary here below which brings God nearer; for me it is everything which keeps him at a distance.' Is not this royal road of salvation which consists of finding and loving God in what is absolutely other than God (the blind necessity of nothingness and evil . . .) strangely like the bare mountain of Carmel where man has as his guide just one single word: nothing? And does Saint John of the Cross speak in less absolute terms of the nothingness of created things and of the love which binds us to them?—'The entire being of the creatures compared with the infinite being of God is nothing, and thus the soul which is a prisoner of what is created is nothing. All the beauty of creatures is supreme ugliness before the infinite beauty of God. All the grace, all the charm of creatures is insipid and repulsive before the divine beauty. All the goodness the creatures contain is only the height of malice when it is in the presence of divine goodness. Only God is good. . . .'

Moreover, though the 'theology' of Simone Weil rejects the idea of popular imagination of a God who governs the world like the father of a family or a temporal sovereign, it does not in any way exclude the action of Providence in the higher sense of the word. There is no doubt that here below matter and evil exercise 'all the causality which belongs to them'; the spectacle of the innumerable horrors of history is enough to prove that the kingdom of God is not of this world (does not Scripture describe the devil as the prince of this world?). Nevertheless God remains mysteriously present in creation: without in any way changing the calamities which weigh upon us, his grace plays upon the laws of gravity like the sun's rays in the clouds. This God 'who is silent in his love' is not indifferent to human misery after the manner of the God of Aristotle or Spinoza. It is out of love for his creature that he appears to efface himself from creation; it is in order to lead him on to the supreme purity that he leaves him to cross the whole expanse of suffering and darkness abandoned and alone. In tying his own hands in the presence of evil, in stripping himself of everything which resembles earthly power and prestige, God invites men to love nothing but love in him. 'He gives himself to men either as powerful or as perfect—it is for them to choose.' But here below infinite perfection is infinite weakness: God, in so far as he is love, hangs wholly and entirely on the Cross. . . .

Simone Weil is not in any way mistaken about the dignity and necessity of temporal values. She sees them as intermediaries— *metaxu*—between the soul and God. 'What is it a sacrilege to destroy? Not that which is base, for that is of no importance. Not that which is high, for we cannot touch that. The *metaxu*. The *metaxu* form the region of good and evil. . . . No human being should be deprived of these *metaxu*, that is to say, of those relative and mixed good things (home, country, traditions, culture, etc.) which warm and nourish the soul and without which, short of sainthood, a human life is not possible.' But these relative and mixed good things can only be treated as such by those who, out of love for God, have passed through the total stripping; all others make them more or less into idols: 'Only he who loves God with a supernatural love can see means simply as means.'

Whatever she may have said about 'choice, a notion of a low

level' and about the absolute fruitlessness of voluntary action in the spiritual domain, Simone Weil does not for all that fall into quietism. On the contrary she constantly recalls that without strict diligence in our practice of the natural virtues, mystical life can be nothing but an illusion. The *cause* of grace dwells outside man, but its *condition* is within him. Simone Weil's hatred for illusion, above all when it takes the form of sensible devotion and a kind of religious *Schwärmerei*, counterbalances everything which in so purified a spirituality might flatter the imagination or the pride. She liked to repeat, after Saint John of the Cross, that inspiration which leads us to neglect the accomplishment of simple and lowly obligations does not come from God. 'Duty is given us in order to kill the self. . . . We only attain to real prayer after we have worn down our own will by keeping rules.'

She regarded with such suspicion any religious exaltation unsupported by a strict fidelity to the daily task that the infrequent negligences of which, largely as a result of her delicate health, she was guilty in the accomplishment of her duties caused her to have bitter doubts about the truth of her spiritual vocation. 'All these mystical phenomena', she wrote at the end of her life with heartrending humility, 'are absolutely beyond me. I do not understand them. They are meant for beings who, to start with, possess the elementary moral virtues. I speak of them at random. And I am not even capable of telling myself sincerely that I speak of them at random.'

Fully sharing the political ideas of Simone Weil as I do, I think it more becoming that I should not dwell on them at great length. Any other person but myself might make something very moving out of the story of this life in which, through the influence of reflection and faith, an essentially revolutionary temperament was gradually impregnated with the cult of tradition and the past. For Simone Weil never ceased to be a revolutionary. She was not however pledged to a chimerical future leading men away from reality, but devoted herself more and more to revolution in the name of an unchanging and eternal principle—a principle which has to be constantly re-established because it constantly tends to be degraded by time. Simone Weil did not believe in an indefinite perfecting of humanity: she even thought that the unfolding of history gave proof of the law of entropy rather than that of unlimited progress after the style of Condorcet. There is no need to defend her on this point. I do not see how it can be heretical to hold (in conformity with the great Greek tradition) that 'change cannot be anything but limited and cyclic'. As for her invectives against the 'social Beast', however excessive a form they may sometimes take we only have to put them back into their context in order to be assured that they do not in any way constitute an apology for anarchy. 'The social order', she writes, 'is irreducibly that of the prince of this world. Our only duty with regard to the social is to try to limit the evil of it. . . . Something of the social labelled divine; an intoxicating mixture which brings about every sort of licence—the devil disguised.' But she adds immediately: 'And yet what about a city? But that is not of the social order—it is a human environment of which we are no more conscious than of the air we breathe—a contact with nature, the past, tradition. A man's roots are not of the social order.' In other words, social influence is both food and poison. It is food in so far as it provides the individual with the inner equipment necessary for living as a man and for approaching God; poison in so far as it tends to rob him of his liberty and to take God's place. The perpetual encroachments of the social order upon the divine—that incessant degradation of mystical conceptions into politics—afford strong enough evidence, today more than ever, of the seriousness of this last danger.

Mutatis mutandis, the same remarks are applicable to the Church. Obviously a spirit so hungering for the absolute as was that of Simone Weil would necessarily be somewhat lacking in a sense of historical relativity: the text *nolite conformari huic a seculo*[1] was for her a commandment allowing of no reservations. She found it very hard to understand that certain concessions of the Church to temporal exigencies did not in any way involve its eternal soul: the beatification of Charlemagne, for instance, seemed to her a scandalous compromise with the social idol. Somewhere she speaks of the Church as 'a great totalitarian beast'. What does that signify? Totalitarianism is characterized at the same time by a refusal of the All and by the claim to be all. As the Catholic Church is the messenger of the All here below it does not need to be totalitarian. The accusation made by Simone Weil, in so far as it is well founded, can therefore only be applicable to certain members of the body of the Church who arbitrarily bolt the doors of love and truth, thus failing to understand the universal vocation of Catholicism. There is no question of reopening here—especially at a time when so many Catholics do not hesitate to provide whips with which to beat their Master—the discussions formerly caused by the idea of 'the Church as a body marked by sin'. We will only state that when Christ said that 'the gates of hell should not prevail', he did not promise that everything in the Church would remain eternally pure, but that the essential deposit of faith would be saved come what might. The Church is rooted in God: that does not exclude the possibility that the tree may bear dried-up or worm-eaten branches. To have faith is to believe that the divine sap will never fail. The preservation of this 'incorruptible core of truth', to use the actual expression of Simone Weil, in the midst of all the impurities mixed into the body of the Church, constitutes moreover one of the strongest proofs of the divinity of Catholicism. The Church could only become a 'great totalitarian beast' in so far as its human body were totally separated from its divine soul. This is an impossible hypothesis, for the gates of hell shall never

[1] 'Be not conformed to this world.'

prevail. . . . Today it is seen as the last refuge of the universal faced with rampant totalitarianisms.

Thus with Simone Weil the expulsion of the social idol does not lead to religious individualism. 'The self and the social are the two great idols.' Grace saves from the one as from the other. That is doubtless what Célestin Bouglé was trying to express in his own manner when he saw in Simone Weil while she was still a student 'a mixture of anarchist and cleric . . .'.

Simone Weil can only be understood on the level from which she speaks. Her work is addressed to souls who, if they are not stripped as naked as her own, have at least kept deep within them an aspiration for that pure goodness to which she devoted her life and her death. I am not unaware of the dangers of a spirituality such as hers. The worst forms of giddiness are caused by the highest summits. But the fact that light may burn us is not a valid reason for leaving it under a bushel.

It is not a question of philosophy here but of life. Far from claiming to set up a personal system, Simone Weil strove with all her power to keep herself out of her work. Her one wish was to avoid getting in the way between God and men—to disappear 'so that the Creator and the creature could exchange their secrets'. She cared nothing for her genius, knowing only too well that true greatness consists in learning to be nothing. 'What does it matter what energy or gifts there may be in me? I have always enough to disappear. . . .' She had her way: some of her texts attain to that impersonal resonance which is the sign of the highest inspiration: 'It is impossible to forgive whoever does us harm if this harm lowers us. We have to think that it does not lower us but that it shows our true level.' Or again: 'If someone does me harm I must want this harm not to degrade me—this out of love for him who inflicted it upon me and so that he shall not really have done harm.' It is in such ejaculations of humility and love rather than on the systematic side of her work that

Simone Weil appears as a pure messenger. I have never ceased to believe in her. In publishing the following pages I extend this confidence to all the souls who shall come to her.

All the writings contained in this book have been taken from the manuscripts which Simone Weil confided to me personally. They were therefore all written before May 1942. More recent work, which her parents have been kind enough to show me, has not been included here. I have myself chosen the extracts from the notebooks, in which they were interspersed with innumerable quotations as well as philological and scientific studies. I hesitated between two ways of presentation: either to give the thoughts of Simone Weil one after the other in the order of their composition, or to classify them. The second method seemed preferable. I am anxious to express my thanks to all who have helped and encouraged me in this work: the Reverend Father Perrin, Lanza del Vasto, M. and Mme Honnorat (who were personal friends of Simone Weil), Gabriel Marcel and Jean de Fabrèques. In the checking and transcription of the texts M. V.-H. Debidour, who kindly helped to translate the Greek quotations incorporated in the aphorisms, and my devoted colleague Mlle Odile Keller have both given an infinite amount of valuable help.

GUSTAVE THIBON
FEBRUARY 1947

GRAVITY AND GRACE

All the *natural* movements of the soul are controlled by laws analogous to those of physical gravity. Grace is the only exception.

We must always expect things to happen in conformity with the laws of gravity unless there is supernatural intervention.

Two forces rule the universe: light and gravity.

Gravity. Generally what we expect of others depends on the effect of gravity upon ourselves, what we receive from them depends on the effect of gravity upon them. Sometimes (by chance) the two coincide, often they do not.

What is the reason that as soon as one human being shows he needs another (no matter whether his need be slight or great) the latter draws back from him? Gravity.

Lear, a tragedy of gravity. Everything we call base is a phenomenon due to gravity. Moreover the word baseness is an indication of this fact.

The object of an action and the level of the energy by which it is carried out are distinct from each other. A certain thing must be done. But where is the energy to be drawn for its accomplishment? A virtuous action can lower a man if there is not enough energy available on the same level.

What is base and what is superficial are on the same level. 'His love is violent but base': a possible sentence. 'His love is deep but base': an impossible one.

If it be true that the same suffering is much harder to bear for a high motive than for a base one (the people who stood, motionless, from one to eight o'clock in the morning for the sake of having an egg, would have found it very difficult to do so in order to save a human life), a base form of virtue is perhaps in some respects better able to stand the test of difficulties, temptations and misfortunes than a noble one. Napoleon's soldiers. Hence the use of cruelty in order to sustain or raise the morale of soldiers. Something not to be forgotten in connexion with moral weakness.

This is a particular example of the law which generally puts force on the side of baseness. Gravity is, as it were, a symbol of it.

Queueing for food. The same action is easier if the motive is base than if it is noble. Base motives have in them more energy than noble ones. Problem: in what way can the energy belonging to the base motives be transferred to the noble ones?

I must not forget that at certain times when my headaches were raging I had an intense longing to make another human being suffer by hitting him in exactly the same part of his forehead.

Analogous desires—very frequent in human beings.

When in this state, I have several times succumbed to the temptation at least to say words which cause pain. Obedience to the force of gravity. The greatest sin. Thus we corrupt the function of language, which is to express the relationship between things.

Attitude of supplication: I must necessarily turn to something other than myself since it is a question of being delivered from self.

Any attempt to gain this deliverance by means of my own energy would be like the efforts of a cow which pulls at its hobble and so falls onto its knees.

In making it one liberates a certain amount of energy in oneself by a violence which serves to degrade more energy. Compensation as in thermodynamics; a vicious circle from which one can be delivered only from on high.

The source of man's moral energy is outside him, like that of his physical energy (food, air etc.). He generally finds it, and that is why he has the illusion—as on the physical plane—that his being carries the principle of its preservation within itself. Privation alone makes him feel his need. And, in the event of privation, he cannot help turning to *anything whatever* which is edible.

There is only one remedy for that: a chlorophyll conferring the faculty of feeding on light.

Not to judge. All faults are the same. There is only one fault: incapacity to feed upon light, for where capacity to do this has been lost all faults are possible.

'My meat is to do the will of Him that sent me.'

There is no good apart from this capacity.

To come down by a movement in which gravity plays no part. . . . Gravity makes things come down, wings make them rise: what wings raised to the second power can make things come down without weight?

Creation is composed of the descending movement of gravity, the ascending movement of grace and the descending movement of the second degree of grace.

Grace is the law of the descending movement.

To lower oneself is to rise in the domain of moral gravity.
Moral gravity makes us fall towards the heights.

Too great affliction places a human being beneath pity: it arouses disgust, horror and scorn.
Pity goes down to a certain level but not below it. What does charity do in order to descend lower?
Have those who have fallen so low pity on themselves?

VOID AND COMPENSATION

Human mechanics. Whoever suffers tries to communicate his suffering (either by ill-treating someone or calling forth their pity) in order to reduce it, and he does really reduce it in this way. In the case of a man in the uttermost depths, whom no one pities, who is without power to ill-treat anyone (if he has no child or being who loves him), the suffering remains within and poisons him.

This is imperative, like gravity. How can one gain deliverance? How gain deliverance from a force which is like gravity?

The tendency to spread evil beyond oneself: I still have it! Beings and things are not sacred enough to me. May I never sully anything, even though I be utterly transformed into mud. To sully nothing, even in thought. Even in my worst moments I would not destroy a Greek statue or a fresco by Giotto. Why anything else then? Why, for example, a moment in the life of a human being who could have been happy for that moment.

It is impossible to forgive whoever has done us harm if that harm has lowered us. We have to think that it has not lowered us, but has revealed our true level.

The wish to see others suffer exactly what we are suffering. It is because of this that, except in periods of social instability, the spite of those in misfortune is directed against their fellows.

That is a factor making for social stability.

The tendency to spread the suffering beyond ourselves. If through excessive weakness we can neither call forth pity nor do harm to others, we attack *what the universe itself represents for us*.

Then every good or beautiful thing is like an insult.

To harm a person is to receive something from him. What? What have we gained (and what will have to be repaid) when we have done harm? We have gained in importance. We have expanded. We have filled an emptiness in ourselves by creating one in somebody else.

To be able to hurt others with impunity—for instance to pass our anger on to an inferior who is obliged to be silent—is to spare ourselves from an expenditure of energy, an expenditure which the other person will have to make. It is the same in the case of the unlawful satisfaction of any desire. The energy we economize in this way is immediately debased.

To forgive. We cannot do this. When we are harmed by someone reactions are set up within us. The desire for vengeance is a desire for essential equilibrium. We must seek equilibrium on another plane. We have to go as far as this limit by ourselves. There we reach the void. (Heaven helps those who help themselves. . . .)

Headaches. At a certain moment, the pain is lessened by projecting it into the universe, but the universe is impaired; the pain is more intense when it comes home again, but something in me does not suffer and remains in contact with a universe which is not impaired. Act in the same way with the passions. Make them come down like a deposit, collect them into a point and become detached from them. Especially, treat all sufferings in this way. Prevent them from having access to things.

The search for equilibrium is bad because it is imaginary. Revenge. Even if in fact we kill or torture our enemy it is, in a sense, imaginary.

A man who lived for his city, his family, his friends, to acquire wealth, improve his social position, etc.—a war: he is led away as a slave and henceforth for evermore he must wear himself out to the utmost limit of his strength merely in order to exist.

That is frightful, impossible, and for this reason he will cling to any aim which presents itself no matter how wretched, be it only to have the slave punished who works at his side. He has no more choice about aims. Any aim at all is like a branch to a drowning man.

Those whose city had been destroyed and who were led away into slavery had no longer either past or future: what had they with which to fill their minds? Lies and the meanest and most pitiful of covetous desires. They were perhaps more ready to risk crucifixion for the sake of stealing a chicken than they had formerly been to risk death in battle for the defence of their town. This is surely so, or those frightful tortures would not have been necessary.

Otherwise they had to be able to endure a void in their minds.

In order to have the strength to contemplate affliction when we are afflicted we need supernatural bread.

A situation which is too hard degrades us through the following process: as a general rule the energy supplied by higher emotions is limited. If the situation requires us to go beyond this limit we have to fall back on lower feelings (fear, covetousness, desire to beat the record, love of outward honours) which are richer in energy.

This limitation is the key to many a retrogression.

Tragedy of those who, having been guided by the love of the Good into a road where suffering has to be endured, after a certain time reach their limit and become debased.

A rock in our path. To hurl ourselves upon this rock as though after a certain intensity of desire had been reached it could not exist any more. Or else to retreat as though we ourselves did not exist. Desire contains something of the absolute and if it fails (once its energy has been used up) the absolute is transferred to the obstacle. This produces the state of mind of the defeated, the oppressed.

To grasp (in each thing) that there is a limit and that without supernatural help that limit cannot be passed—or only by very little and at the price of a terrible fall afterwards.

Energy, freed by the disappearance of the objects which provide motives, always tends to go downwards.

Base feelings (envy, resentment) are degraded energy.

Every kind of reward constitutes a degradation of energy.

Self-satisfaction over a good action (or a work of art) is a degradation of higher energy. That is why the left hand should not know . . .

A purely imaginary reward (a smile from Louis XIV) is the exact equivalent of what we have expended, for it has exactly the same value as what we have expended—unlike real rewards which, as such, are either of higher or lower value. Hence *imaginary advantages* alone supply the energy for unlimited effort. But it is necessary that Louis XIV should really smile; if he does not, it is an unutterable deprivation. A king can only pay out imaginary rewards most of the time or he would be insolvent.

It is the same with religion at a certain level. Instead of receiving the smile of Louis XIV, we invent a God who smiles on us.

Or again we praise ourselves. There must be an equivalent reward. This is as inevitable as gravity.

A beloved being who disappoints me. I have written to him. It is impossible that he should not reply by saying what I have said to myself in his name.

Men owe us what we imagine they will give us. We must forgive them this debt.

To accept the fact that they are other than the creatures of our imagination is to imitate the renunciation of God.

I also am other than what I imagine myself to be. To know this is forgiveness.

TO ACCEPT THE VOID

'Tradition teaches us as touching the gods and experience shows us as regards men that, by a necessity of nature, every being invariably exercises all the power of which it is capable' (Thucydides). Like a gas, the soul tends to fill the entire space which is given it. A gas which contracted leaving a vacuum—this would be contrary to the law of entropy. It is not so with the God of the Christians. He is a *supernatural* God, whereas Jehovah is a *natural* God.

Not to exercise all the power at one's disposal is to endure the void. This is contrary to all the laws of nature. Grace alone can do it.

Grace fills empty spaces but it can only enter where there is a void to receive it, and it is grace itself which makes this void.

The necessity for a reward, the need to receive the equivalent of what we give. But if, doing violence to this necessity, we leave a vacuum, as it were a suction of air is produced and a supernatural reward results. It does not come if we receive other wages: it is this vacuum which makes it come.

It is the same with the remission of debts (and this applies not only to the harm which others have done us but to the good which we have done them). There again, we accept a void in ourselves.

To accept a void in ourselves is supernatural. Where is the energy to be found for an act which has nothing to counterbalance it? The energy has to come from elsewhere. Yet first there must be a tearing out, something desperate has to take place, the void must be created. Void: the dark night.

Admiration, pity (most of all a mixture of the two) bring real energy. But this we must do without.

A time has to be gone through without any reward, natural or supernatural.

The world must be regarded as containing something of a void in order that it may have need of God. That presupposes evil.

To love truth means to endure the void and, as a result, to accept death. Truth is on the side of death.

Man only escapes from the laws of this world in lightning flashes. Instants when everything stands still, instants of contemplation, of pure intuition, of mental void, of acceptance of the moral void. It is through such instants that he is capable of the supernatural.

Whoever endures a moment of the void either receives the supernatural bread or falls. It is a terrible risk, but one that must be run—even during the instant when hope fails. But we must not throw ourselves into it.

DETACHMENT

Affliction in itself is not enough for the attainment of total detachment. Unconsoled affliction is necessary. There must be no consolation—no apparent consolation. Ineffable consolation then comes down.

To forgive debts. To accept the past without asking for future compensation. To stop time at the present instant. This is also the acceptance of death.

'He emptied himself of his divinity.' To empty ourselves of the world. To take the form of a slave. To reduce ourselves to the point we occupy in space and time—that is to say, to nothing.

To strip ourselves of the imaginary royalty of the world. Absolute solitude. Then we possess the truth of the world.

Two ways of renouncing material possessions:

To give them up with a view to some spiritual advantage.

To conceive of them and feel them as conducive to spiritual well-being (for example: hunger, fatigue and humiliation cloud the mind and hinder meditation) and yet to renounce them.

Only the second kind of renunciation means nakedness of spirit.

Furthermore, material goods would scarcely be dangerous if they were seen in isolation and not bound up with spiritual advantage.

We must give up everything which is not grace and not even desire grace.

The extinction of desire (Buddhism)—or detachment—or *amor fati*—or desire for the absolute good—these all amount to the same: to empty desire, finality of all content, to desire in the void, to desire without any wishes.

To detach our desire from all good things and to wait. Experience proves that this waiting is satisfied. It is then we touch the absolute good.

Always, beyond the particular object whatever it may be, we have to fix our will on the void—to will the void. For the good which we can neither picture nor define is a void for us. But this void is fuller than all fullnesses.

If we get as far as this we shall come through all right, for God fills the void. It has nothing to do with an intellectual process in the present-day sense. The intelligence has nothing to discover, it has only to clear the ground. It is only good for servile tasks.

The good seems to us as a nothingness, since there is no thing that is good. But this nothingness is not unreal. Compared with it, everything in existence is unreal.

We must leave on one side the beliefs which fill up voids and sweeten what is bitter. The belief in immortality. The belief in the utility of sin: *etiam peccata*. The belief in the providential ordering of events—in short the 'consolations' which are ordinarily sought in religion.

To love God through and across the destruction of Troy and of Carthage—and with no consolation. Love is not consolation, it is light.

The reality of the world is the result of our attachment. It is the reality of the self which we transfer into things. It has nothing to do with independent reality. That is only perceptible through total detachment. Should only one thread remain, there is still attachment.

Affliction which forces us to attach ourselves to the most wretched objects exposes in all its misery the true character of attachment. In this way the necessity for detachment is made more obvious.

Attachment is a manufacturer of illusions and whoever wants reality ought to be detached.

As soon as we know that something is real we can no longer be attached to it.

Attachment is no more nor less than an insufficiency in our sense of reality. We are attached to the possession of a thing because we think that if we cease to possess it, it will cease to exist. A great many people do not feel with their whole soul that there is all the difference in the world between the destruction of a town and their own irremediable exile from that town.

Human misery would be intolerable if it were not diluted in time. We have to prevent it from being diluted in order that it should be intolerable.

'And when they had had their fill of tears' (Iliad).—This is another way of making the worst suffering bearable.

We must not weep so that we may not be comforted.[1]

---

[1] Yet Jesus Christ said: 'Blessed are they that mourn'. But here Simone Weil is only condemning the tears wrung from us by the loss of temporal goods—tears which man sheds over himself.   [Editor's note.]

All suffering which does not detach us is wasted suffering. Nothing is more frightful, a desolate coldness, a warped soul (Ovid. Slaves in Plautus).

Never to think of a thing or being we love but have not actually before our eyes without reflecting that perhaps this thing has been destroyed, or this person is dead.

May our sense of reality not be dissolved by this thought but made more intense.

Each time that we say 'Thy will be done' we should have in mind all possible misfortunes added together.

Two ways of killing ourselves: suicide or detachment.

To kill by our thought everything we love: the only way to die. Only what we love, however ('He who hateth not his father and mother . . .' but: 'Love your enemies . . .').

Not to desire that what we love should be immortal. We should neither desire the immortality nor the death of any human being, whoever he may be, with whom we have to do.

The miser deprives himself of his treasure because of his desire for it. If we can let our whole good rest with something hidden in the ground, why not with God?

But when God has become as full of significance as the treasure is for the miser, we have to tell ourselves insistently that he does not exist. We must experience the fact that we love him, even if he does not exist.

It is he who, through the operation of the dark night, withdraws himself in order not to be loved like the treasure is by the miser.

Electra weeping for the dead Orestes. If we love God while thinking that he does not exist, he will manifest his existence.

IMAGINATION WHICH FILLS
THE VOID

The imagination is continually at work filling up all the fissures through which grace might pass.

Every void (not accepted) produces hatred, sourness, bitterness, spite. The evil we wish for that which we hate, and which we imagine, restores the balance.

The militiamen of the *Spanish Testament* who invented victories in order to endure death: an example of imagination filling up the void. Although we should gain nothing by the victory, we can bear to die for a cause which is going to triumph, not for one which will be defeated. For something absolutely denuded of power, it would be superhuman (the disciples of Christ). The thought of death calls for a counterweight, and this counterweight—apart from grace—cannot be anything but a lie.

The imagination, filler up of the void, is essentially a liar. It does away with the third dimension, for only real objects have three dimensions. It does away with multiple relationships.

To try to define the things which, while they do indeed happen, yet remain in a sense imaginary. War. Crimes. Acts of revenge. Extreme affliction.

The crimes in Spain were actually perpetrated and yet they resembled mere acts of boastfulness.

Realities which have no more dimensions than a dream.

In the case of evil, as in that of dreams, there are not multiple readings.[1] Hence the simplicity of criminals.

Crimes flat like dreams on both sides: on the side of the executioner and on the side of the victim. What is more frightful than to die in a nightmare?

Compensations. Marius imagined future retribution. Napoleon thought of posterity. William II wanted a cup of tea. His imagination was not strongly enough attached to power to be able to span the years: it turned towards a cup of tea.

The adoration of the great by the people in the seventeenth century (La Bruyère). This was a result of imagination filling up the void, a result which has disappeared since money has been substituted for it. Two base results, but money the baser of the two.

In no matter what circumstances, if the imagination is stopped from pouring itself out we have a void (the poor in spirit).

In no matter what circumstances (but sometimes at the price of how great a degradation!) imagination can fill the void. This is why average human beings can become prisoners, slaves,

---

[1] For the meaning of this word (lectures) in the vocabulary of Simone Weil, see later chapter on Readings.

prostitutes and pass through no matter what suffering without being purified.

We must continually suspend the work of the imagination filling the void within ourselves.

If we accept no matter what void, what stroke of fate can prevent us from loving the universe?

We have the assurance that, come what may, *the universe is full.*

RENUNCIATION OF TIME

Time is an image of eternity, but it is also a substitute for eternity.

The miser whose treasure has been taken from him. It is some of the frozen past which he has lost. Past and future, man's only riches.

The future is a filler of void places. Sometimes the past also plays this part ('I used to be,' 'I once did this or that . . .'). But there are other cases when affliction makes the thought of happiness intolerable; then it robs the sufferer of his past (*nessun maggior dolore* . . .).

The past and the future hinder the wholesome effect of affliction by providing an unlimited field for imaginary elevation. That is why the renunciation of past and future is the first of all renunciations.

The present does not attain finality. Nor does the future, for it is only what will be present. We do not know this, however. If we apply to the present the point of that desire within us which corresponds to finality, it pierces right through to the eternal.

That is the use of despair which turns the attention away from the future.

When we are disappointed by a pleasure which we have been expecting and which comes, the disappointment is because we were expecting the future, and as soon as it is there it is present. We want the future to be there without ceasing to be future. This is an absurdity of which eternity alone is the cure.

Time and the cave. To come out of the cave, to be detached, means to cease to make the future our objective.

A method of purification: to pray to God, not only in secret as far as men are concerned, but with the thought that God does not exist.[1]

Piety with regard to the dead: to do everything for what does not exist.

The suffering caused by the death of others is due to this pain of a void and of lost equilibrium. Efforts henceforward follow without an object and therefore without a reward. If the imagination makes good this void—debasement. 'Let the dead bury their dead.' And as to our own death, is it not the same? The object and the reward are in the future. Deprivation of the future—void, loss of equilibrium. That is why 'to philosophise is to learn to die'. That is why 'to pray is like a death'.

[1] God does not in fact exist in the same way as created things which form the only object of experience for our *natural* faculties. Therefore, contact with supernatural reality is at first felt as an experience of nothingness.   [Editor's note.]

When pain and weariness reach the point of causing a sense of perpetuity to be born in the soul, through contemplating this perpetuity with acceptance and love, we are snatched away into eternity.

TO DESIRE WITHOUT AN OBJECT

Purification is the separation of good from covetousness.

We have to go down to the root of our desires in order to tear the energy from its object. That is where the desires are true in so far as they are energy. It is the object which is unreal. But there is an unspeakable wrench in the soul at the separation of a desire from its object.

If we go down into ourselves we find that we possess exactly what we desire.

If we long for a certain being (who is dead), we desire a particular, limited being; therefore, necessarily, a mortal, and we long for that special being 'who' . . . 'to whom' . . ., etc., in short that being who died at such and such a time on such and such a day. And we have that being—dead.

If we desire money, we want a medium of exchange (institution), something which can only be acquired on certain conditions, so we desire it only 'in the measure that' . . . Well, in that measure we have it.

In such cases suffering, emptiness are the mode of existence of the objects of our desire. We only have to draw aside the veil of unreality and we shall see that they are given to us in this way.

When we see that, we still suffer, but we are happy.

To ascertain exactly what the miser whose treasure was stolen lost: thus we should learn much.

Lauzun and the office of Captain of Musketeers. He preferred to be a prisoner and Captain of Musketeers rather than to go free and not be Captain.

These are garments. 'They were ashamed of their nakedness.'

To lose someone: we suffer because the departed, the absent, has become something imaginary and unreal. But our desire for him is not imaginary. We have to go down into ourselves to the abode of the desire which is not imaginary. Hunger: we imagine kinds of food, but the hunger itself is real: we have to fasten on to the hunger. The presence of the dead person is imaginary, but his absence is very real: henceforward it is his way of appearing.

We must not seek the void, for it would be tempting God if we counted on supernatural bread to fill it.

We must not run away from it either.

The void is the supreme fullness, but man is not permitted to know it. The proof is that Christ himself was at one moment completely unaware of it. One part of the self should know it, but not the other parts, for if they knew it in their base fashion, there would no longer be any void.

Christ experienced all human misery, except sin. But he experienced everything which makes man capable of sin. It is the void which makes man capable of sin. All sins are attempts to fill voids. Thus my life with all its stains is near to his perfectly pure one, and the same is true of much lower lives. However low I fall I shall not go very far from him. But if I fall I shall no longer be able to know this.

The handshake of a friend on meeting again after a long absence. I do not even notice whether it gives pleasure or pain to my sense of touch: like the blind man who feels the objects directly at the end of his stick, I feel the presence of my friend directly. It is the same with life's circumstances, whatever they may be, and God.

This implies that we should never seek consolation for pain. Because felicity is beyond the realm of consolation and pain. We become aware of it through a sense which is different, just as the perception of objects at the end of a stick or an instrument is different from touch in the strict sense of the word. This other sense is formed by a shifting of the attention through an apprenticeship in which the whole soul and body participate.

That is why we read in the Gospel: 'I say to you that these have received their reward.' There must be no compensation. It is the void in our sensibility which carries us beyond sensibility.

Denial of Saint Peter. To say to Christ: 'I will never deny Thee' was to deny him already, for it was supposing the source of faithfulness to be in himself and not in grace. Happily, as he was chosen, this denial was made manifest to all and to himself. How many others boast in the same way—and they never understand.

It was difficult to be faithful to Christ. A fidelity in the void was needed. It was much easier to be faithful to Napoleon, even if it involved death. It was easier for the martyrs to be Faithful, later on, because the Church was already there, a force with temporal promises. We die for what is strong, not for what is weak, or only for what is weak momentarily and has still kept an aureole of strength. Faithfulness to Napoleon at Saint-Helena was not faithfulness in the void. The fact of dying for what is strong robs death of its bitterness—and at the same time of all its value.

To implore a man is a desperate attempt through sheer intensity to make our system of values pass into him. To implore God is just the contrary: it is an attempt to make the divine values pass into ourselves. Far from thinking with all the intensity of which we are capable of the values to which we are attached, we must preserve an interior void.

THE SELF

We possess nothing in the world—a mere chance can strip us of everything—except the power to say 'I'. That is what we have to give to God—in other words, to destroy. There is absolutely no other free act which it is given us to accomplish—only the destruction of the 'I'.

Offering: We cannot offer anything but the 'I', and all we call an offering is merely a label attached to a compensatory assertion of the 'I'.

Nothing in the world can rob us of the power to say 'I'. Nothing except extreme affliction. Nothing is worse than extreme affliction which destroys the 'I' from outside, because after that we can no longer destroy it ourselves. What happens to those whose 'I' has been destroyed from outside by affliction? It is not possible to imagine anything for them but annihilation according to the atheistic or materialistic conception.

Though they may have lost their 'I', it does not mean that they have no more egoism. Quite the reverse. To be sure, this may occasionally happen when a dog-like devotion is brought about, but at other times the being is reduced to naked, vegetative egoism. An egoism without an 'I'.

So long as we ourselves have begun the process of destroying the 'I', we can prevent any affliction from causing harm. For the 'I' is not destroyed by external pressure without a violent revolt. If for the love of God we refuse to give ourselves over to this revolt, the destruction does not take place from outside but from within.

Redemptive suffering. If a human being who is in a state of perfection and has through grace completely destroyed the 'I' in himself, falls into that degree of affliction which corresponds for him to the destruction of the 'I' from outside—we have there the cross in its fullness. Affliction can no longer destroy the 'I' in him for the 'I' in him no longer exists, having completely disappeared and left the place to God. But affliction produces an effect which is equivalent, on the plane of perfection, to the exterior destruction of the 'I'. It produces the absence of God. 'My God, why hast Thou forsaken me?'

What is this absence of God produced by extreme affliction within the perfect soul? What is the value which is attached to it and which is known as redemptive suffering?

Redemptive suffering is that by which evil really has fullness of being to the utmost extent of its capacity.

By redemptive suffering, God is present in extreme evil. For the absence of God is the mode of divine presence which corresponds to evil—absence which is felt. He who has not God within himself cannot feel his absence.

It is the purity, the perfection, the plenitude, the abyss of evil. Whereas hell is a false abyss (cf. Thibon). Hell is superficial. Hell is a nothingness which has the pretension and gives the illusion of being.

Purely external destruction of the 'I' is quasi-infernal suffering. External destruction with which the soul associates itself through love is expiatory suffering. The bringing about of the absence of God in a soul completely emptied of self through love is redemptive suffering.

In affliction the vital instinct survives all the attachments which have been torn away, and blindly fastens itself to everything which can provide it with support, like a plant fastens its tendrils. Gratitude (except in a base form) and justice are not conceivable in this state. Slavery. There is no longer the extra amount of energy required to support free-will by which man takes the measure of things. Affliction, from this point of view, is hideous as life in its nakedness always is, like an amputated stump, like the swarming of insects. Life without form. Survival is then the only attachment. That is where extreme affliction begins—when all other attachments are replaced by that of survival. Attachment appears then in its nakedness without any other object but itself—Hell.

It is by this mechanism that to those in affliction life appears as the one thing desirable, at the very time when their life is in no way preferable to death.

In this state, to accept death is total detachment.

Quasi-hell on earth. Complete uprooting in affliction

Human injustice as a general rule produces not martyrs but quasi-damned souls. Beings who have fallen into this quasi-hell are like someone stripped and wounded by robbers. They have lost the clothing of character.

The greatest suffering which allows any of a man's roots to remain is at an infinite distance from this quasi-hell.

When we do a service to beings thus uprooted and we receive in exchange discourtesy, ingratitude, betrayal, we are merely enduring a small share of their affliction. It is our duty to expose ourselves to it in a limited measure just as it is our duty to expose ourselves to affliction. When it comes we should endure it as we endure affliction, without referring it back to particular people, for it cannot be referred back to anything. There is something impersonal in quasi-infernal affliction as there is in perfection.

For those whose 'I' is dead we can do nothing, absolutely nothing. We never know, however, whether in a particular person the 'I' is quite dead or only inanimate. If it is not quite dead, love can reanimate it as though by an injection, but it must be love which is utterly pure without the slightest trace of condescension, for the least shade of contempt drives towards death.

When the 'I' is wounded from outside it starts by revolting in the most extreme and bitter manner like an animal at bay. But as soon as the 'I' is half dead, it wants to be finished off and allows itself to sink into unconsciousness. If it is then awakened by a touch of love, there is sharp pain which results in anger and sometimes hatred for whoever has provoked this pain. Hence the apparently inexplicable vindictiveness of the fallen towards their benefactors.

It can also happen that the love of the benefactor is not pure. Then, in the 'I', awakened by love but immediately wounded afresh by contempt, there surges up the bitterest of hatreds, a hatred which is legitimate.

He, on the contrary, in whom the 'I' is quite dead is in no way embarrassed by the love which is shown him. He takes what comes just as dogs and cats receive food, warmth and caresses, and, like them, he is eager to obtain as much as possible. As the case may be, he either attaches himself like a dog or accepts what comes to him with a certain indifference like a cat. Without the slightest scruple he absorbs all the energy of whoever tries to help him.

Unfortunately in every charitable work there is a danger lest the majority of its clients should be composed of people with no scruples, and above all, of people in whom the 'I' has been killed.

The weaker the character of him who endures affliction, the more quickly is the 'I' destroyed. To be more exact, the limit of the affliction which destroys the 'I' is situated at a greater or lesser distance according to the quality of the character, and the further it is the more the character is said to be strong.

The position of this limit, whether near or far, is probably a fact of nature in the same way as a gift for mathematics, and he who, without having any faith, is proud of preserving his morale in difficult circumstances, has no more reason to be so than the youth who is conceited because mathematics come easily to him. He who believes in God is in danger of a still greater illusion—that of attributing to grace what is simply an essentially mechanical effect of nature.

The agony of extreme affliction is the destruction of the 'I' from outside: Arnolphe, Phèdre, Lycaon. We are right to fall on our knees, to make abject supplication when that violent death which is going to strike us down threatens to kill the 'I' from outside even before life is destroyed.

'Niobe also, of the beautiful hair, thought of eating.' That is sublime, in the same way as space in Giotto's frescoes.

A humiliation which forces us to renounce even despair.

The sin in me says 'I'.

I am all. But this particular 'I' is God. And it is not an 'I'.

Evil makes distinctions, it prevents God from being equivalent to all.

It is because of my wretchedness that I am 'I'. It is on account of the wretchedness of the universe that, in a sense, God is 'I' (that is to say a person).

The Pharisees were people who relied on their own strength to be virtuous.

Humility consists in knowing that in what we call 'I' there is no source of energy by which we can rise.

Everything without exception which is of value in me comes from somewhere other than myself, not as a gift but as a loan which must be ceaselessly renewed. Everything without exception which is in me is absolutely valueless; and, among the gifts which have come to me from elsewhere, everything which I appropriate becomes valueless immediately I do so.

Perfect joy excludes even the very feeling of joy, for in the soul filled by the object no corner is left for saying 'I'.

We cannot imagine such joys when they are absent, thus the incentive for seeking them is lacking.

DECREATION

Decreation: to make something created pass into the uncreated.

Destruction: to make something created pass into nothingness A blameworthy substitute for decreation.

Creation is an act of love and it is perpetual. At each moment our existence is God's love for us. But God can only love himself. His love for us is love for himself through us. Thus, he who gives us our being loves in us the acceptance of not being.

Our existence is made up only of his waiting for our acceptance not to exist. He is perpetually begging from us that existence which he gives. He gives it to us in order to beg it from us.

Relentless necessity, wretchedness, distress, the crushing burden of poverty and of labour which wears us out, cruelty, torture, violent death, constraint, disease—all these constitute divine love. It is God who in love withdraws from us so that we can love him. For if we were exposed to the direct radiance of his love, without the protection of space, of time and of matter, we should be evaporated like water in the sun; there would not be enough 'I' in us to make it possible to surrender the 'I' for love's sake. Necessity is the screen set between God and us so that we can be. It is for us to pierce through the screen so that we cease to be.

There exists a 'deifugal' force. Otherwise all would be God.

An imaginary divinity has been given to man so that he may strip himself of it like Christ did of his real divinity.

Renunciation. Imitation of God's renunciation in creation. In a sense God renounces being everything. We should renounce being something. That is our only good.

We are like barrels with no bottom to them so long as we have not understood that we have a base.

Elevation and abasement. A woman looking at herself in a mirror and adorning herself does not feel the shame of reducing the self, that infinite being which surveys all things, to a small space. In the same way every time that we raise the ego (the social ego, the psychological ego etc.) as high as we raise it, we degrade ourselves to an infinite degree by confining ourselves to being no more than that. When the ego is abased (unless energy tends to raise it by desire), we know that we are not that.

A very beautiful woman who looks at her reflection in the mirror can very well believe that she is that. An ugly woman knows that she is not that.

Everything which is grasped by our natural faculties is hypothetical. It is only supernatural love that establishes anything. Thus we are co-creators.

We participate in the creation of the world by decreating ourselves.

We only possess what we renounce; what we do not renounce escapes from us. In this sense, we cannot possess anything whatever unless it passes through God.

Catholic communion. God did not only make himself flesh for us once, every day he makes himself matter in order to give himself to man and to be consumed by him. Reciprocally, by fatigue, affliction and death, man is made matter and is consumed by God. How can we refuse this reciprocity?

He emptied himself of his divinity. We should empty ourselves of the false divinity with which we were born.
  Once we have understood we are nothing, the object of all our efforts is to become nothing. It is for this that we suffer with resignation, it is for this that we act, it is for this that we pray.
  May God grant me to become nothing.
  In so far as I become nothing, God loves himself through me.

There is a resemblance between the lower and the higher. Hence slavery is an image of obedience to God, humiliation an image of humility, physical necessity an image of the irresistible pressure of grace, the saints' self-abandonment from day to day an image of the frittering away of time among criminals, prostitutes, etc.
  On this account it is necessary to seek out what is lowest, as an image.
  May that which is low in us go downwards so that what is high can go upwards. For we are wrong side upward. We are born thus. To re-establish order is to undo the creature in us.

Reversal of the objective and the subjective.
  Similarly, reversal of the positive and the negative. That is also the meaning of the philosophy of the Upanishads.
  We are born and live in an inverted fashion, for we are born

and live in sin which is an inversion of the hierarchy. The first operation is one of reversal—Conversion.

Except the seed die. . . . It has to die in order to liberate the energy it bears within it so that with this energy new forms may be developed.
So we have to die in order to liberate a tied up energy, in order to possess an energy which is free and capable of understanding the true relationship of things.

The extreme difficulty which I often experience in carrying out the slightest action is a favour granted to me. For thus, by ordinary actions and without attracting attention, I can cut some of the roots of the tree. However indifferent we may be to the opinion of others, extraordinary actions contain a stimulus which cannot be separated from them. This stimulus is quite absent from ordinary actions. To find extraordinary difficulty in doing an ordinary action is a favour which calls for gratitude. We must not ask for the removal of such a difficulty: we must beg for grace to make good use of it.

In general we must not wish for the disappearance of any of our troubles, but grace to transform them.

For men of courage physical sufferings (and privations) are often a test of endurance and of strength of soul. But there is a better use to be made of them. For me then, may they not be that. May they rather be a testimony, lived and felt, of human misery. May I endure them in a completely passive manner. Whatever happens, how could I ever think an affliction too great, since the wound of an affliction and the abasement to which those whom it strikes are condemned opens to them the knowledge of human misery, knowledge which is the door of all wisdom?
But pleasure, happiness, prosperity, if we know how to

recognize in them all that comes from outside (chance, circumstances, etc.), likewise bear testimony to human misery. They should be used in the same way. This applies even to grace, in so far as it is a sensible phenomenon.

We have to be nothing in order to be in our right place in the whole.

Renunciation demands that we should pass through anguish equivalent to that which would be caused in reality by the loss of all loved beings and all possession, including our faculties and attainments in the order of intelligence and character, our opinions, beliefs concerning what is good, what is stable, etc. And we must not lay these things down of ourselves but lose them—like Job. Moreover the energy thus cut off from its object should not be wasted in oscillations and degraded. The anguish should therefore be still greater than in real affliction, it should not be cut up and spread over time nor oriented towards a hope.

When the passion of love goes as far as vegetative energy, then we have cases like Phèdre, Arnolphe, etc.: 'Et je sens là dedans qu'il faudra que je crève. . . .'[1]

Hippolyte is really more necessary to the life of Phèdre, in the most literal sense of the word, than food.

In order that the love of God may penetrate as far down as that, nature has to undergo the ultimate violence. Job, the cross. . . .

The love of Phèdre or of Arnolphe is impure. A love which should descend as low as theirs and yet remain pure. . . . We must become nothing, we must go down to the vegetative level; it is then that God becomes bread.

If we consider what we are at a definite moment—the present

---

[1] 'And I feel that I must die of it. . . .'

moment, cut off from the past and the future—we are innocent. We cannot at that instant be anything but what we are: all progress implies duration. It is in the order of the world at this instant that we should be such as we are.

To isolate a moment in this way implies pardon. But such isolation is detachment.

There are only two instants of perfect nudity and purity in human life: birth and death. It is only when newly-born or on our death-bed that we can adore God in human form without sullying the divinity.

Death. An instantaneous state, without past or future. Indispensable for entering eternity.

If we find fullness of joy in the thought that God is, we must find the same fullness in the knowledge that we ourselves are not, for it is the same thought. And this knowledge is extended to our sensibility only through suffering and death.

Joy within God. Perfect and infinite joy really exists within God. My participation can add nothing to it, my non-participation can take nothing from the reality of this perfect and infinite joy. Of what importance is it then whether I am to share in it or not? Of no importance whatever.

Those who wish for their salvation do not truly believe in the reality of the joy within God.

Belief in immortality is harmful because it is not in our power to conceive of the soul as really incorporeal. So this belief is in fact a belief in the prolongation of life, and it robs death of its purpose.

The presence of God. This should be understood in two ways. As Creator, God is present in everything which exists as soon as it exists. The presence for which God needs the co-operation of the creature is the presence of God, not as Creator but as Spirit. The first presence is the presence of creation. The second is the presence of decreation. (He who created us without our help will not save us without our consent. Saint Augustine.)

God could create only by hiding himself. Otherwise there would be nothing but himself.

Holiness should then be hidden too, even from consciousness in a certain measure. And it should be hidden in the world.

Being and having. Being does not belong to man, only having. The being of man is situated behind the curtain, on the supernatural side. What he can know of himself is only what is lent him by circumstances. My 'I' is hidden for me (and for others); it is on the side of God, it is in God, it is God. To be proud is to forget that one is God. . . . The curtain is human misery: there was a curtain even for Christ.

Job. Satan to God: 'Doth he love Thee for thyself alone?' It is a question of the level of love. Is love situated on the level of sheep, fields of corn, numerous children? Or is it situated further off, in the third dimension, behind? However deep this love may be there is a breaking-point when it succumbs, and it is this moment which transforms, which wrenches us away from the finite towards the infinite, which makes the soul's love for God transcendent in the soul. It is the death of the soul. Woe to him for whom the death of the body precedes that of the soul. The soul which is not full of love dies a bad death. Why is it necessary that such a death should happen without distinction. It must indeed be so. It is necessary that everything should happen without distinction.

Appearance clings to being, and pain alone can tear them from each other.

For whoever is in possession of being there can be no appearance. Appearance chains being down.

Time in its course tears appearance from being and being from appearance by violence. Time makes it manifest that it is not eternity.

It is necessary to uproot oneself. To cut down the tree and make of it a cross, and then to carry it every day.

It is necessary not to be 'myself', still less to be 'ourselves'.
The city gives us the feeling of being at home.
We must take the feeling of being at home into exile.
We must be rooted in the absence of a place.

To uproot oneself socially and vegetatively.
To exile oneself from every earthly country.
To do all that to others, from the outside, is a substitute (*ersatz*) for decreation. It results in unreality.
But by uprooting oneself one seeks greater reality.

SELF-EFFACEMENT

God gave me being in order that I should give it back to him. It is like one of those traps whereby the characters are tested in fairy stories and tales on initiation. If I accept this gift it is bad and fatal; its virtue becomes apparent through my refusal of it. God allows me to exist outside himself. It is for me to refuse this authorization.

Humility is the refusal to exist outside God. It is the queen of virtues.

The self is only the shadow which sin and error cast by stopping the light of God, and I take this shadow for a being.

Even if we could be like God it would be better to be mud which obeys God.

To be what the pencil is for me when, blindfold, I feel the table by means of its point—to be that for Christ. It is possible for us to be mediators between God and the part of creation which is confided to us. Our consent is necessary in order that he may perceive his own creation through us. With our consent he performs this marvel. If I knew how to withdraw from my own soul it would be enough to enable this table in front of me to have the incomparable good fortune of being seen by God. God can love in us only this consent to withdraw in order to make way for him, just as he himself, our creator, withdrew in order that we might come into being. This double operation has no other meaning than love, it is like a father giving his child something which will enable the child to give a present on his father's birthday. God who is no other thing but love has not created anything other than love.

All the things that I see, hear, breathe, touch, eat; all the beings I meet—I deprive the sum total of all that of contact with God, and I deprive God of contact with all that in so far as something in me says 'I'.

I can do something for all that and for God—namely, retire and respect the *tête-à-tête*.

The strict carrying out of ordinary human duty is a condition which makes my withdrawal possible. Little by little it wears away the ropes which fasten me to the spot and prevent me from retiring.

I cannot conceive the necessity for God to love me, when I feel so clearly that even with human beings affection for me can only be a mistake. But I can easily imagine that he loves that perspective of creation which can only be seen from the point where I am. But I act as a screen. I must withdraw so that he may see it.

I must withdraw so that God may make contact with the beings whom chance places in my path and whom he loves. It is tactless for me to be there. It is as though I were placed between two lovers or two friends. I am not the maiden who awaits her betrothed, but the unwelcome third who is with two betrothed lovers and ought to go away so that they can really be together.

If only I knew how to disappear there would be a perfect union of love between God and the earth I tread, the sea I hear . . .

What do the energy, the gifts, etc. which are in me matter? I always have enough of them to disappear.

'Et la mort à mes yeux ravissant la clarté
Rend au jour qu'ils souillaient toute sa pureté. . . .'[1]

May I disappear in order that those things that I see may become perfect in their beauty from the very fact that they are no longer things that I see.

I do not in the least wish that this created world should fade from my view, but that it should no longer be to me personally that it shows itself. To me it cannot tell its secret which is too high. If I go, then the creator and the creature will exchange their secrets.

To see a landscape as it is when I am not there. . . .

When I am in any place, I disturb the silence of heaven and earth by my breathing and the beating of my heart.

---

[1]   'And death, robbing my eyes of their light,
Restores to the day they sullied all in purity . . .

NECESSITY AND OBEDIENCE

The sun shines on the just and on the unjust. . . . God makes himself *necessity*. There are two aspects of necessity: it is exercised, it is endured: the sun and the cross.

We have to consent to be subject to necessity and to act only by handling it.

Subordination: economy of energy. Thanks to this, an act of heroism can be performed without there being any need for the person who commands or the one who obeys to be a hero.

We have to attain to receiving orders from God.

In which cases does the struggle against temptation exhaust the energy attached to goodness and in which cases does it make it rise higher in the scale of qualities of energy?

This must depend on the respective importance of the parts played by the will and the attention.

We have to deserve, by the strength of our love, to suffer constraint.

Obedience is the supreme virtue. We have to love necessity. Necessity is what is lowest in relation to the individual (constraint, force, a 'hard fate'); universal necessity brings deliverance from this.

There are cases where a thing is necessary from the mere fact that it is possible. Thus to eat when we are hungry, to give a wounded man, dying of thirst, something to drink when there is water quite near. Neither a ruffian nor a saint would refrain from doing so.

By analogy, we have to discern the cases in which, although it does not appear so clearly at first sight, the possibility implies a necessity, we must act in these cases and not in the others.

The pomegranate seed. We do not pledge ourselves to love God, we give our consent to the engagement which has been formed within us in spite of ourselves.

We should do only those righteous actions which we cannot stop ourselves from doing, which we are unable not to do, but, through well directed attention, we should always keep on increasing the number of those which we are unable not to do.

We should not take one step, *even in the direction of what is good*, beyond that to which we are irresistibly impelled by God, and this applies to action, word and thought. But we should be willing to go anywhere under his impulsion, even to the farthest limit (the cross). . . . To be willing to go as far as possible is to pray to be impelled, but without knowing whither.

If my eternal salvation were on this table in the form of an object and if I only had to stretch out my hand to grasp it, I would not stretch out my hand without having received orders to do so.

Detachment from the fruits of action. To escape from inevitability of this kind. How? To act not for an object but from necessity. I cannot do otherwise. It is not an action but a sort of passivity. Inactive action.

The slave is in a sense a model (the lowest . . . the highest . . . always this same law). So also is matter.

To transfer the source of our actions outside ourselves. To be impelled. The purest of motives (or the basest: the law is always the same) appear as something *exterior*.

Every act should be considered from the point of view not of its object but of its impulsion. The question is not 'What is the aim?' It is 'What is the origin?'

'I was naked, and ye clothed me.' This gift is simply an indication of the state of those who acted in this way. They were in a state which made it impossible for them not to feed the hungry and to clothe the naked; they did not in any way do it for Christ, they could not help doing it because the compassion of Christ was in them. It was the same with Saint Nicholas who, when going across the Russian Steppes with Saint Cassian to meet God, could not help being late for the appointed time of meeting because he had to help a poor peasant to move his cart which had stuck in the mud. Good which is done in this way, almost in spite of ourselves, almost shamefacedly and apologetically, is pure. All absolutely pure goodness completely eludes the will. Goodness is transcendent. God is Goodness.

'I was an hungred, and ye gave me meat.' When was that, Lord? They did not know. We must not know when we do such acts.

We must not help our neighbour for Christ but in Christ. May

the self disappear in such a way that Christ can help our neighbour through the medium of our soul and body. May we be the
slave whom his master sends to bear help to someone in misfortune. The help comes from the master, but it is intended for
the sufferer. Christ did not suffer for his Father. He suffered
for men by the Father's will.

We cannot say of the slave who goes off bearing help that he is
doing it for his master. He is doing nothing. Even though in
order to reach the sufferer he had to walk barefoot over nails, he
would suffer but he would not be doing anything. For he is a
slave.

'We are unprofitable servants': that means we have done
nothing.

In general the expression 'for God' is a bad one. God ought
not to be put in the dative.

We should not go to our neighbour for the sake of God, but
we should be impelled towards our neighbour by God, as the
arrow is driven towards its target by the archer.

To be only an intermediary between the uncultivated ground
and the ploughed field, between the data of a problem and the
solution, between the blank page and the poem, between the
starving beggar and the beggar who has been fed.

With all things, it is always what comes to us from outside, freely
and by surprise as a gift from heaven, without our having sought
it, that brings us pure joy. In the same way real good can only
come from outside ourselves, never from our own effort. We
cannot under any circumstances manufacture something which
is better than ourselves. Thus effort truly stretched towards
goodness cannot reach its goal; it is after long, fruitless effort
which ends in despair, when we no longer expect anything, that,
from outside ourselves, the gift comes as a marvellous surprise.
The effort has destroyed a part of the false sense of fullness

within us. The divine emptiness, fuller than fullness, has come to inhabit us.

The will of God. How to know it? If we make a quietness within ourselves, if we silence all desires and opinions and if with love, without formulating any words, we bind our whole soul to think 'Thy will be done', the thing which after that we feel sure we should do (even though in certain respects we may be mistaken) is the will of God. For if we ask him for bread he will not give us a stone.

Convergency as a criterion. An action or attitude for which reason affords several distinct and convergent motives, but which we feel transcends all imaginable motives.

In prayer we must not have in view any particular thing, unless by supernatural inspiration, for God is the universal being. To be sure, he descends into the realm of particular things. He has descended, he descends in the act of creation; as also in the Incarnation, the Eucharist, Inspiration, etc. But the movement comes from above, never from below; it is a movement on God's part, not on ours. We cannot bring about such intercommunion except when God decrees it. Our rôle is to be ever turned towards the universal.

There perhaps we have the solution to Berger's difficulty about the impossibility of a union between the relative and the absolute. It cannot be achieved by a movement rising from below, but it is possible by a descending movement from on high.

We can never know that God commands a certain thing. Intention directed towards obedience to God saves us, whatever we do, if we place God infinitely above us, and damns us, whatever we do, if we call our own heart God. In the first case we never think what we have done, what we are doing or what we are going to do can be good.

The use of temptations. It depends on the relative strength of the soul and of time. To go on for a long time contemplating the possibility of doing evil without doing it effects a kind of transubstantiation. If we resist with merely finite energy, this energy is exhausted after a certain time, and when it is exhausted we give in. If we remain motionless and attentive it is the temptation which is exhausted—and we acquire the energy raised to a higher degree.

If, in the same way—that is to say motionless and attentive— we contemplate the possibility of doing good, a transubstantiation of energy is brought about in this case also, and thanks to it we accomplish the good we have been considering.

The transubstantiation of the energy consists in the fact that, where what is good is concerned, a moment comes when we cannot help doing it.

This, moreover, provides a criterion of good and evil.

Every creature which attains perfect obedience constitutes a special, unique, irreplaceable form of the presence, knowledge and operation of God in the world.

Necessity. We have to see things in their right relationship and ourselves, including the purposes we bear within us, as one of the terms of that relationship. Action follows naturally from this.

Obedience. There are two kinds. We can obey the force of gravity or we can obey the relationship of things. In the first case we do what we are driven to by the imagination which fills up empty spaces. We can affix a variety of labels to it, often with a show of truth, including righteousness and God. if we suspend the filling up activity of the imagination and fix our attention on the relationship of things, a necessity becomes apparent which we cannot help obeying. Until then we have not any notion of necessity and we have no sense of obedience.

After that we cannot be proud of what we do, even though we may accomplish marvels.

The words of the Breton ship's boy to the journalist who asked him how he had been able to act as he did: 'There was nothing else for it'—the purest heroism—more frequent among the poor than elsewhere.

Obedience is the only pure motive, the only one which does not in the slightest degree seek a reward for the action, but leaves all care of reward to the Father who is in secret and who sees in secret.

The obedience must, however, be obedience to necessity and not to force (terrible void in the case of slaves).

However much we give of ourselves to others or to a great cause, whatever suffering we endure, if it is out of pure obedience to a clear conception of the relationship of things and to necessity, we make up our minds to it without effort although we accomplish it with effort. We cannot do otherwise, and there is no reversal, no void to be filled, no thought of reward, no spite, no loss of dignity.

Action is the pointer of the balance. We must not touch the pointer but the weight.

Exactly the same rule applies to opinions.

If we fail to observe it there is either confusion or suffering.

The Foolish Virgins—The meaning of this story is that at the moment when we become conscious that we have to make a choice, the choice is already made for good or ill. This is much truer than the allegory about Hercules between virtue and vice.

When the inward nature of man, cut off from all carnal

influences and deprived of all supernatural light, performs actions which are in conformity with those which supernatural light would impose if it were present, there is utter purity. That is the central point of the Passion.

In contemplation, the right relationship with God is love, in action it is slavery. This distinction must be kept. We must act as becomes a slave while contemplating with love. . . .

ILLUSIONS

We are drawn towards a thing because we believe it is good. We end by being chained to it because it has become necessary.

Things of the senses are real if they are considered as perceptible things, but unreal if considered as goods.

Appearance has the completeness of reality, but only as appearance. As anything other than appearance it is error.

Illusions about the things of this world do not concern their existence but their value. The image of the cave refers to values. We only possess shadowy imitations of good. It is also in relation to good that we are chained down like captives (attachment). We accept the false values which appear to us and when we think we are acting we are in reality motionless, for we are still confined in the same system of values.

Actions effectively carried out and yet imaginary. A man

attempts suicide, recovers and is no more detached afterwards than he was before. His suicide was imaginary. Suicide is probably never anything else, and that is why it is forbidden.

Strictly speaking time does not exist (except within the limit of the present), yet we have to submit to it. Such is our condition. *We are subject to that which does not exist.* Whether it is a question of passively borne duration—physical pain, waiting, regret, remorse, fear—or of organized time—order, method, necessity—in both cases that to which we are subject does not exist. But our submission exists. We are really bound by unreal chains. Time which is unreal casts over all things including ourselves a veil of unreality.

The miser's treasure is the shadow of an imitation of what is good. It is doubly unreal. For, to start with, a means to an end (such as money) is, in itself, something other than a good. But diverted from its function as a means and set up as an end, it is still further from being a good.

It is with regard to the assessment of values that our sense-perceptions are unreal, since things are unreal for us as values. But to attribute a false value to an object also takes reality from the perception of this object, because it submerges perception in imagination.

Thus perfect detachment alone enables us to see things in their naked reality, outside the fog of deceptive values. That is why ulcers and the dung-heap were necessary before Job could receive the revelation of the world's beauty. For there is no detachment where there is no pain. And there is no pain endured without hatred or lying unless detachment is present also.

The soul which has poked its head out of heaven devours the being. The soul which has remained inside devours opinion.

Necessity is essentially a stranger to the imaginary.

What is real in perception and distinguishes it from dreams is not the sensations, but the *necessity* enshrined in these sensations.
'Why these things and not others?'
'Because that is how it is.'
In the spiritual life illusion and truth are distinguished in the same way.
What is real in perception and distinguishes it from dreams is not sensations but necessity.
There is a distinction between those who remain inside the cave, shutting their eyes and imagining the journey, and those who really take it. In the spiritual realm also we have real and imaginary, and there also it is *necessity* which makes the difference—not simply suffering, because there are imaginary sufferings. As for inner feelings, nothing is more deceptive.

How can we distinguish the imaginary from the real in the spiritual realm?
We must prefer real hell to an imaginary paradise.

That which distinguishes higher states from lower ones is the coexistence in the higher states of several superposed planes.

Humility has as its object to eliminate that which is imaginary in spiritual progress. There is no harm in thinking ourselves far less advanced than we are: the effect of the light is in no way decreased thereby for its source is not in opinion. There is great harm in thinking ourselves more advanced, because then opinion has an effect.

A test of what is real is that it is hard and rough. Joys are found in it, not pleasure. What is pleasant belongs to dreams.

We must try to love without imagining—to love the appearance in its nakedness without interpretation. What we love then is truly God.

After having experienced the absolute good, we find the illusory and partial aspects of goods once more, but in a hierarchical order, so that we only allow ourselves to seek one such aspect within a limit where it does not interfere with the care due to another. This order is transcendent in relation to the aspects of goods which it connects together and it is a reflection of the absolute good.

Already discursive reason (the understanding of relationships) helps to break down idolatries by considering good and evil things as limited, merging, overlapping.

We must recognize the point at which good passes into evil: in so far as, to the extent that, having regard to, etc.

We must get further than the rule of three.

There is always a relationship to time to be taken into account. We must get rid of the illusion of possessing time. We must become incarnate.

Man has to perform an act of incarnation, for he is disembodied (désincarné) by his imagination. What comes to us from Satan is our imagination.

Cure for imaginary love. To give God the strict minimum in us, what it is absolutely impossible for us to refuse him—and desire that one day, and as soon as possible, this strict minimum may become all.

Transposition: we believe we are rising because while keeping the same base inclinations (for instance; the desire to triumph over others) we have given them a noble object.

We should, on the contrary, rise by attaching noble inclinations to lowly objects.

All the passions produce prodigies. A gambler is capable of watching and fasting almost like a saint, he has his premonitions, etc.

There is great danger in loving God as the gambler loves his game.

We must be careful about the level on which we place the infinite. If we place it on the level which is only suitable for the finite it will matter very little what name we give it.

The lower parts of my nature should love God, but not too much, for then it would not be God.

May their love be like hunger and thirst. Only the highest has the right to be satisfied.

Fear of God in Saint John of the Cross. Is this not the fear of thinking about God when we are unworthy; of sullying him by thinking about him wrongly? Through such fear the lower parts of our nature draw away from God.

The flesh is dangerous in so far as it refuses to love God, but also in so far as without fitting modesty it pushes itself forward to love him.

Why is the determination to fight against a prejudice a sure sign that one is full of it? Such a determination necessarily arises from an obsession. It constitutes an utterly sterile effort to get rid of it. In such a case the light of attention is the only thing which is effective, and it is not compatible with a polemical intention.

All the Freudian system is impregnated with the prejudice which it makes it its mission to fight—the prejudice that everything sexual is vile.

There is an essential difference between the mysticism which turns towards God the faculty of love and desire of which sexual energy constitutes the physiological foundation, and the false imitation of mysticism which, without changing the natural orientation of this faculty, gives it an imaginary object upon which it stamps the name of God as a label. To discriminate between these two operations, of which the second is still lower than debauchery, is difficult, but it is possible.

God and the supernatural are hidden and formless in the universe. It is well that they should be hidden and nameless in the soul. Otherwise there would be a risk of having something imaginary under the name of God (those who fed and clothed Christ did not know that it was Christ). This is the meaning of the ancient mysteries. Christianity (Catholic and Protestant) speaks too much about holy things.

Morality and literature. Imagination and fiction go to make up more than three-quarters of our real life. Rare indeed are the true contacts with good and evil.

A science which does not bring us nearer to God is worthless.
But if it brings us to him in the wrong way, that is to say if it brings us to an imaginary God, it is worse. . . .

It is bad to think that I am the author of the operations which nature mechanically performs in me: it is still worse to think that the Holy Spirit is the author of them. That is still farther from the truth.

Different types of correlation and passage from one opposite to another:
Through total devotion to something great (including God), giving free licence to our lower nature.
Through contemplation of the infinite distance between the

self and what is great, making of the self an instrument of greatness.

By what criterion can they be distinguished?

I think the only criterion is that bad correlation removes the limits from that which is rightly limited.

If we except the highest forms of sanctity and genius, that which gives the impression of being true in man is almost bound to be false, and that which is true is almost bound to give the impression of being false.

Work is needed to express what is true: also to receive what is true. We can express and receive what is false, or at least what is superficial, without any work.

When truth appears at least as true as falsehood it is a triumph of sanctity or of genius. Thus Saint Francis made his audience cry just like a cheap theatrical preacher would have done.

Duration, whether of centuries in the case of civilizations or of years and decades for individuals, has the Darwinian function of eliminating the unfit. That which is fitted for all things is eternal. In this alone lies the value of what we call experience. But falsehood is an armour by means of which man often enables what is unfit in him to survive events which, were it not for such armour, would destroy it (thus pride manages to survive humiliations), and this armour is as it were secreted by what is unfit in order to ward off the danger (in humiliation, pride makes thicker the inner falsehood which covers it). There is as it were a phagocytosis in the soul: everything which is threatened by time secretes falsehood in order not to die, and in proportion to the danger it is in of dying. That is why there is not any love of truth without an unconditional acceptance of death. The cross of Christ is the only gateway to knowledge.

I should look upon every sin I have committed as a favour of

God. It is a favour that the essential imperfection which is hidden in my depths should have been to some extent made dear to me on a certain day, at a certain time, in certain circumstances. I wish and implore that my imperfection may be wholly revealed to me in so far as human thought is capable of grasping it. Not in order that it may be cured but, even if it should not be cured, in order that I may know the truth.

Everything that is worthless shuns the light. Here on earth we can hide ourselves beneath the flesh. At death we can do this no longer. We are given up naked to the light. That means hell, purgatory or paradise as the case may be.

That which makes us hold back from the effort which would bring us nearer to what is good is the repugnance of the flesh, but it is not the flesh's repugnance in the face of effort. It is the flesh's repugnance in the face of what is good, because for a bad cause, if there were a strong enough incentive, the flesh would consent to anything, knowing it could do so without dying. Death itself, endured for a bad cause, is not really death for the carnal part of the soul. What is mortal for the carnal part of the soul is to see God face to face.

That is why we fly from the inner void since God might steal into it.

It is not the pursuit of pleasure and the aversion for effort which causes sin, but fear of God. We know that we cannot see him face to face without dying and we do not want to die. We know that sin preserves us very effectively from seeing him face to face: pleasure and pain merely provide us with the slight indispensable impetus towards sin, and above all the pretext or alibi which is still more indispensable. In the same way as pretexts are necessary for unjust wars, a promise of some false good is necessary for sin, because we cannot endure the thought that we are going in the direction of evil. It is not the flesh which keeps us away from God; the flesh is the veil we place before us to shield us from him.

This is perhaps not the case until after a certain point has been reached. The image of the cave seems to suggest as much. At first it is movement which hurts. When we reach the opening it is the light. It not only blinds but wounds us. Our eyes turn away from it.

May it not be true that from that moment onwards mortal sins are the only kind we can any longer commit?

To use the flesh to hide ourselves from the light—is not that a mortal sin? A horrible idea.

Leprosy is preferable.

I need God to take me by force, because, if death, doing away with the shield of the flesh, were to put me face to face with him, I should run away.

IDOLATRY

Idolatry comes from the fact that, while thirsting for absolute good, we do not possess the power of supernatural attention and we have not the patience to allow it to develop.

Lacking idols, it often happens that we have to labour every day, or nearly every day, in the void. We cannot do so without supernatural bread.

Idolatry is thus a vital necessity in the cave. Even with the best of us it is inevitable that it should set narrow limits for mind and heart.

Ideas are changeable, they are influenced by the passions, by fancy, by fatigue. Activity has to be constant. It has to continue each day and for many hours each day. Motives for our activity are therefore needed which shall be independent of our thoughts, hence of our relationships: idols.

All men are ready to die for what they love. They differ only through the level of the thing loved and the concentration or diffusion of their love. No one loves himself.

Man would like to be an egoist and cannot. This is the most striking characteristic of his wretchedness and the source of his greatness.

Man always devotes himself to an *order*. Only, unless there is supernatural illumination, this order has as its centre either himself or some particular being or thing (possibly an abstraction) with which he has identified himself (e.g. Napoleon, for his soldiers, Science, or some political party, etc.). It is a perspective order.

We do not have to acquire humility. There is humility in us— only we humiliate ourselves before false gods.

LOVE

Love is a sign of our wretchedness. God can only love himself. We can only love something else.

God's love for us is not the reason for which we should love him. God's love for us is the reason for us to love ourselves. How could we love ourselves without this motive?

It is impossible for man to love himself except in this roundabout way.

If my eyes are blindfolded and if my hands are chained to a stick, this stick separates me from things but I can explore them by means of it. It is only the stick which I feel, it is only the wall which I perceive. It is the same with creatures and the faculty of love. Supernatural love touches only creatures and goes only to God. It is only creatures which it loves (what else have we to love?), but it loves them as intermediaries. For this reason it loves all creatures equally, itself included. To love a stranger as oneself implies the reverse: to love oneself as a stranger.

Love of God is pure when joy and suffering inspire an equal degree of gratitude.

Love on the part of someone who is happy is the wish to share the suffering of the beloved who is unhappy.

Love on the part of someone who is unhappy is to be filled with joy by the mere knowledge that his beloved is happy without sharing in this happiness or even wishing to do so.

In Plato's eyes, carnal love is a degraded image of true love. Chaste human love (conjugal fidelity) is a less degraded image of it. Only in the stupidity of the present day could the idea of sublimation arise.

The Love of Phaedrus. He neither exercises force nor submits to it. That constitutes the only purity. Contact with the sword causes the same defilement whether it be through the handle or the point. For him who loves, its metallic coldness will not destroy love, but will give the impression of being abandoned by God. Supernatural love has no contact with force, but at the same time it does not protect the soul against the coldness of force, the coldness of steel. Only an earthly attachment, if it has in it enough energy, can afford protection from the coldness of steel. Armour, like the sword, is made of metal. Murder freezes the soul of the man who loves only with a pure love, whether he be the author or the victim, so likewise does everything which, without going so far as actual death, constitutes violence. If we want to have a love which will protect the soul from wounds, we must love something other than God.

Love tends to go ever further and further, but there is a limit. When the limit is passed love turns to hate. To avoid this change love has to become different.

Among human beings, only the existence of those we love is fully recognized.

Belief in the existence of other human beings as such is love.

The mind, is not forced to believe in the existence of anything (subjectivism, absolute idealism, solipsism, scepticism: c.f. the Upanishads, the Taoists and Plato, who, all of them, adopt this philosophical attitude by way of purification). That is why the only organ of contact with existence is acceptance, love. That is why beauty and reality are identical. That is why joy and the sense of reality are identical.

This need to be the creator of what we love is a need to imitate God. But the divinity towards which it tends is false, unless we have recourse to the model seen from the other, the heavenly side. . . .

Pure love of creatures is not love in God, but love which has passed through God as through fire. Love which detaches itself completely from creatures to ascend to God and comes down again associated with the creative love of God.

Thus the two opposites which rend human love are united: to love the beloved being just as he is, and to want to recreate him.

Imaginary love of creatures. We are attached by a cord to all the objects of attachment, and a cord can always be cut. We are also attached by a cord to the imaginary God, the God for whom love is also an attachment. But to the real God we are not attached and that is why there is no cord which can be cut. He enters into us. He alone can enter into us. All other things remain outside and our knowledge of them is confined to the tensions of varying degree and direction which affect the cord when there is a change of position on their part or on ours.

Love needs reality. What is more terrible than the discovery that through a bodily appearance we have been loving an imaginary being. It is much more terrible than death, for death does not prevent the beloved from having lived.

That is the punishment for having fed love on imagination.

It is an act of cowardice to seek from (or to wish to give) the people we love any other consolation than that which works of art give us. These help us through the mere fact that they exist. To love and to be loved only serves mutually to render this existence more concrete, more constantly present to the mind. But it should be present as the source of our thoughts, not as their object. If there are grounds for wishing to be understood, it is not for ourselves but for the other, in order that we may exist for him.

Everything which is vile or second-rate in us revolts against purity and needs, in order to save its own life, to soil this purity.

To soil is to modify, it is to touch. The beautiful is that which we cannot wish to change. To assume power over is to soil. To possess is to soil.

To love purely is to consent to distance, it is to adore the distance between ourselves and that which we love.

The imagination is always united with a desire, that is to say a value. Only desire without an object is empty of imagination. There is the real presence of God in everything which imagination does not veil. The beautiful takes our desire captive and empties it of its object, giving it an object which is present and thus forbidding it to fly off towards the future.

Such is the price of chaste love. Every desire for enjoyment belongs to the future and the world of illusion, whereas if we desire only that a being should exist, he exists: what more is there to desire? The beloved being is then naked and real, not veiled by an imaginary future. The miser never looks at his treasure without imagining it n times larger. It is necessary to be dead in order to see things in their nakedness.

Thus in love there is chastity or the lack of chastity according to whether the desire is or is not directed towards the future.

In this sense, and on condition that it is not turned towards a pseudo-immortality conceived on the model of the future, the love we devote to the dead is perfectly pure. For it is the desire for a life which is finished, which can no longer give anything new. We desire that the dead man should have existed, and he has existed.

Wherever the spirit ceases to be a principle it also ceases to be an end. Hence the close connexion between collective 'thought' under all its forms and the loss of the sense of and respect for souls. The soul is the human being considered as having a value in itself. To love the soul of a woman is not to think of her a serving one's own pleasure, etc. Love no longer knows how to contemplate, it wants to possess (disappearance of Platonic love).[1]

It is a fault to wish to be understood before we have made ourselves clear to ourselves. It is to seek pleasures in friendship and pleasures which are not deserved. It is something which corrupts even more than love. You would sell your soul for friendship.

Learn to thrust friendship aside, or rather the dream of friend-

---

[1] Here 'Platonic' love has nothing to do with what today goes by the same name. It does not proceed from the imagination but from the soul. It is purely spiritual contemplation. Cf. later, in the chapter on Beauty.   [Editor's note.]

ship. To desire friendship is a great fault. Friendship should be a gratuitous joy like those afforded by art or life. We must refuse it so that we may be worthy to receive it; it is of the order of grace ('Depart from me, O Lord. . . .'). It is one of those things which are added unto us. *Every* dream of friendship deserves to be shattered. It is not by chance that you have never been loved. . . . To wish to escape from solitude is cowardice. Friendship is not to be sought, not to be dreamed, not to be desired; it is to be exercised (it is a virtue). We must have done with all this impure and turbid border of sentiment. Schluss!

Or rather (for we must not prune too severely within ourselves), everything in friendship which does not pass into real exchanges should pass into considered thoughts. It serves no useful purpose to do without the inspiring virtue of friendship. What should be severely forbidden is to dream of its sentimental joys. That is corruption. Moreover it is as stupid as to dream about music or painting. Friendship cannot be separated from reality any more than the beautiful. It is a miracle, like the beautiful. And the miracle consists simply in the fact that it *exists*. At the age of twenty-five, it is high time to have done with adolescence once and for all. . . .

Do not allow yourself to be imprisoned by any affection. Keep your solitude. The day, if it ever comes, when you are given true affection there will be no opposition between interior solitude and friendship, quite the reverse. It is even by this infallible sign that you will recognize it. Other affections have to be severely disciplined.

The same words (e.g. a man says to his wife: 'I love you') can be commonplace or extraordinary according to the manner in which they are spoken. And this manner depends on the depth of the region in a man's being from which they proceed without the will being able to do anything. And by a marvellous agreement they reach the same region in him who hears them. Thus the hearer can discern, if he has any power of discernment, what is the value of the words.

Benefaction is permissible precisely because it constitutes a humiliation still greater than pain, a still more intimate and undeniable proof of dependence. And gratitude is prescribed for the same reason, since therein lies the use to be made of the received benefit. The dependence, however, must be on fate and not on any particular human being. That is why the benefactor is under an obligation to keep himself entirely out of the benefaction. Moreover the gratitude must not in any degree constitute an attachment, for that is the gratitude proper to dogs.

Gratitude is first of all the business of him who helps, if the help is pure. It is only by virtue of reciprocity that it is due from him who is helped.

In order to feel true gratitude (the case of friendship being set aside), I have to think that it is not out of pity, sympathy or caprice that I am being treated well, it is not as a favour or privilege, nor as a natural result of temperament, but from a desire to do what justice demands. Accordingly he who treats me thus wishes that all who are in my situation may be treated in the same way by all who are in his own.

EVIL

Creation: good broken up into pieces and scattered throughout evil.

Evil is limitless but it is not infinite. Only the infinite limits the limitless.

Monotony of evil: never anything new, everything about it is equivalent. Never anything real, everything about it is imaginary.

It is because of this monotony that quantity plays so great a part. A host of women (Don Juan) or of men (Célimène), etc. One is condemned to false infinity. That is hell itself.

Evil is licence and that is why it is monotonous: everything has to be drawn from ourselves. But it is not given to man to create, so it is a bad attempt to imitate God.

Not to recognize and accept this impossibility of creating is the source of many an error. We are obliged to imitate the act of creation, and there are two possible imitations—the one real and the other apparent—preserving and destroying.

There is no trace of 'I' in the act of preserving. There is in that of destroying. The 'I' leaves its mark on the world as it destroys.

Literature and morality. Imaginary evil is romantic and varied; real evil is gloomy, monotonous, barren, boring. Imaginary good is boring; real good is always new, marvellous, intoxicating. Therefore 'imaginative literature' is either boring or immoral (or a mixture of both). It only escapes from this alternative if in some way it passes over to the side of reality through the power of art—and only genius can do that.

A certain inferior kind of virtue is good's degraded image, of which we have to repent, and of which it is more difficult to repent than it is of evil—The Pharisee and the Publican.

Good as the opposite of evil is, in a sense, equivalent to it, as is the way with all opposites.

It is not good which evil violates, for good is inviolate: only a degraded good can be violated.

That which is the direct opposite of an evil never belongs to the order of higher good. It is often scarcely any higher than evil! Examples: theft and the bourgeois respect for property, adultery and the 'respectable woman'; the savings-bank and waste; lying and 'sincerity'.

Good is essentially other than evil. Evil is multifarious and fragmentary, good is one, evil is apparent, good is mysterious; evil consists in action, good in non-action, in activity which does not act, etc.—Good considered on the level of evil and measured against it as one opposite against another is good of the penal code order. Above there is a good which, in a sense, bears more resemblance to evil than to this low form of good. This fact opens the way to a great deal of demagogy and many tedious paradoxes.

Good which is defined in the way in which one defines evil should be rejected. Evil does reject it. But the way it rejects it is evil.

Is there a union of incompatible vices in beings given over to evil? I do not think so. Vices are subject to gravity and that is why there is no depth or transcendence in evil.

We experience good only by doing it.

We experience evil only by refusing to allow ourselves to do it, or, if we do it, by repenting of it.

When we do evil we do not know it, because evil flies from the light.

Does evil, as we conceive it to be when we do not do it, exist? Does not the evil that we do seem to be something simple and natural which compels us? Is not evil analogous to illusion? When we are the victims of an illusion we do not feel it to be an illusion but a reality. It is the same perhaps with evil. Evil when we are in its power is not felt as evil but as a necessity, or even a duty.

As soon as we do evil, the evil appears as a sort of duty. Most people have a sense of duty about doing certain things that are bad and others that are good. The same man feels it to be a duty to sell for the highest price he can and not to steal etc. Good for such people is on the level of evil, it is a good without light.

The sensitivity of the innocent victim who suffers is like felt crime. True crime cannot be felt. The innocent victim who suffers knows the truth about his executioner, the executioner does not know it. The evil which the innocent victim feels in himself is in his executioner, but he is not sensible of the fact. The innocent victim can only know the evil in the form of suffering. That which is not felt by the criminal is his own crime. That which is not felt by the innocent victim is his own innocence.

It is the innocent victim who can feel hell.

The sin which we have in us emerges from us and spreads outside ourselves setting up a contagion of sin. Thus, when we are in a temper, those around us grow angry. Or again, from superior to inferior: anger produces fear. But at the contact of a perfectly pure being there is a transmutation and the sin becomes suffering. Such is the function of the just servant of Isaiah, of the Lamb of God. Such is redemptive suffering. All the criminal violence of the Roman Empire ran up against Christ and in him it became pure suffering. Evil beings, on the other hand, transform simple suffering (sickness for example) into sin.

It follows, perhaps, that redemptive suffering has to have a social origin. It has to be injustice, violence on the part of human beings.

The false God changes suffering into violence. The true God changes violence into suffering.

Expiatory suffering is the shock in return for the evil we have done. Redemptive suffering is the shadow of the pure good we desire.

A hurtful act is the transference to others of the degradation which we bear in ourselves. That is why we are inclined to commit such acts as a way of deliverance.

All crime is a transference of the evil in him who acts to him who undergoes the result of the action. This is true of unlawful love as well as murder.

The apparatus of penal justice has been so contaminated with evil, after all the centuries during which it has, without any compensatory purification, been in contact with evil-doers, that a condemnation is very often a transference of evil from the penal apparatus itself to the condemned man; and that is possible even when he is guilty and the punishment is not out of proportion. Hardened criminals are the only people to whom the penal apparatus can do no harm. It does terrible harm to the innocent.

When there is a transference of evil, the evil is not diminished but increased in him from whom it proceeds. This is a phenomenon of multiplication. The same is true when the evil is transferred to things.

Where, then, are we to put the evil?

We have to transfer it from the impure part to the pure part of ourselves, thus changing it into pure suffering. The crime which is latent in us we must inflict on ourselves.

In this way, however, it would not take us long to sully our own point of inward purity if we did not renew it by contact with an unchangeable purity placed beyond all possible attack.

Patience consists in not transforming suffering into crime. That in itself is enough to transform crime into suffering.

To transfer evil to what is exterior is to distort the relationship between things. That which is exact and fixed, number, proportion, harmony, withstands this distortion. Whatever my state, whether vigorous or exhausted, in three miles there are three milestones. That is why number hurts when we are suffering: it interferes with the operation of transference. To fix my attention on what is too rigid to be distorted by my interior modifications is to prepare to make possible within myself the apparition of something changeless and an access to the eternal.

We must accept the evil done to us as a remedy for that which we have done.

It is not the suffering we inflict on ourselves but that which comes to us from outside which is the true remedy. Moreover, it has to be unjust. When we have sinned by injustice it is not enough to suffer what is just, we have to suffer injustice.

Purity is absolutely invulnerable as purity, in the sense that no violence can make it less pure. It is, however, highly vulnerable in the sense that every attack of evil makes it suffer, that every sin which touches it turns in it to suffering.

If someone does me an injury I must desire that this injury shall not degrade me. I must desire this out of love for him who inflicts it, in order that he may not really have done evil.

The saints (those who are nearly saints) are more exposed than others to the devil because the real knowledge they have of their wretchedness makes the light almost intolerable.

The sin against the Spirit consists of knowing a thing to be good and hating it because it is good. We experience the equivalent of it in the form of resistance every time we set our faces in the direction of good. For every contact with good leads to a knowledge of the distance between good and evil and the commencement of a painful effort of assimilation. It is something which hurts and we are afraid. This fear is perhaps the sign of the reality of the contact. The corresponding sin cannot come about unless a lack of hope makes the consciousness of the distance intolerable and changes the pain into hatred. Hope is a remedy in this respect, but a better remedy is indifference to ourselves and happiness because the good is good although we are far from it and may even suppose that we are destined to remain separated from it for ever.

Once an atom of pure good has entered the soul the most criminal weakness is infinitely less dangerous than the very slightest treason, even though this should be confined to a purely inward movement of thought lasting no more than an instant but to which we have given our consent. That is a participation in hell. So long as the soul has not tasted of pure goodness it is separated from hell as it is from paradise.

It is only possible to choose hell through an attachment to salvation. He who does not desire the joy of God but is satisfied to know that there really is joy in God, falls but does not commit treason.

When we love God through evil as such, it is really God whom we love.

We have to love God through evil as such: to love God through the evil we hate, while hating this evil: to love God as the author of the evil which we are actually hating.

Evil is to love, what mystery is to the intelligence. As mystery compels the virtue of faith to be supernatural, so does evil the virtue of charity. Moreover, to try to find compensation or justification for evil is just as harmful for charity as to try to expose the content of the mysteries on the plane of human intelligence.

Speech of Ivan in the *Karamazovs*: 'Even though this immense factory were to produce the most extraordinary marvels and were to cost only a single tear from a single child, I refuse.'

I am in complete agreement with this sentiment. No reason whatever which anyone could produce to compensate for a child's tear would make me consent to that tear. Absolutely none which the mind can conceive. There is just one, however, but it is intelligible only to supernatural love: 'God willed it'. And for that reason I would consent to a world which was nothing but evil as readily as to a child's tear.

The death agony is the supreme dark night which is necessary even for the perfect if they are to attain to absolute purity, and for that reason it is better that it should be bitter.

The unreality which takes the goodness from good; this is what constitutes evil. Evil is always the destruction of tangible things in which there is the real presence of good. Evil is carried out by those who have no knowledge of this real presence. In that sense it is true that no one is wicked voluntarily. The relations between forces give to absence the power to destroy presence.

We cannot contemplate without terror the extent of the evil which man can do and endure.

How could we believe it possible to find a compensation for this evil, since because of it God suffered crucifixion?

Good and evil. Reality. That which gives more reality to beings and things is good, that which takes it from them is evil.

The Romans did evil by robbing the Greek towns of their statues, because the towns, the temples and the life of the Greeks had less reality without the statues, and because the statues could not have as much reality in Rome as in Greece.

The desperate, humble supplication of the Greeks to be allowed to keep some of their statues—a desperate attempt to make their own notion of value pass into the minds of others. Understood this, there is nothing base in their behaviour. But it was almost bound to be ineffectual. There is a duty to understand and weigh the system of other people's values with our own, on the same balance—to forge the balance.

To allow the imagination to dwell on what is evil implies a

certain cowardice; we hope to enjoy, to know and to grow through what is unreal.

Even to dwell in imagination on certain things as possible (quite a different thing from clearly conceiving the possibility of them, which is essential to virtue) is to commit ourselves to them already. Curiosity is the cause of it. We have to forbid ourselves certain things (not the conception of them but the dwelling on them): we must not think about them. We believe that thought does not commit us in any way, but it alone commits us, and licence of thought includes all licence. Not to think about a thing—supreme faculty. Purity—negative virtue. If we have allowed our imagination to dwell on an evil thing, if we meet other men who make it objective through their words and actions and thus remove the social barrier, we are already nearly lost. And what is easier? There is no sharp division. When we see the ditch we are already over it. With good it is quite otherwise; the ditch is visible when it has still to be crossed, at the moment of the wrench and the rending. One does not fall into good. The word baseness (lowness) expresses this property of evil.

Even when it is an accomplished fact evil keeps the character of unreality; this perhaps explains the simplicity of criminals; everything is simple in dreams. This simplicity corresponds to that of the highest virtue.

Evil has to be purified—or life is not possible. God alone can do that. This is the idea of the Gita. It is also the idea of Moses, of Mahomet, of Hitlerism . . .

But Jehovah, Allah, Hitler are earthly Gods. The purification they bring about is imaginary.

That which is essentially different from evil is virtue accompanied by a dear perception of the possibility of evil and of evil appearing as something good. The presence of illusions which we have abandoned but which are still present in the mind is perhaps the criterion of truth.

We cannot have a horror of doing harm to others unless we have reached a point where others can no longer do harm to us (then we love others, to the furthest limit, like our past selves).

The contemplation of human misery wrenches us in the direction of God, and it is only in others whom we love as ourselves that we can contemplate it. We can neither contemplate it in ourselves as such nor in others as such.

The extreme affliction which overtakes human beings does not create human misery, it merely reveals it.

Sin and the glamour of force. Because the soul in its entirety has not been able to know and accept human misery, we think that there is a difference between human beings, and in this way we fall short of justice, either by making a difference between ourselves and others or by making a selection among others.

This is because we do not know that human misery is a constant and irreducible quantity which is as great as it can be in each man, and that greatness comes from the one and only God, so that there is identity between one man and another in this respect.

We are surprised that affliction does not have an ennobling effect. This is because when we think of the afflicted person it is the affliction we have in mind. Whereas he himself does not think of his affliction: he has his soul filled with no matter what paltry comfort he may have set his heart on.

How could there be no evil in the world? The world has to be foreign to our desires. If this were so without it containing evil, our desires would then be entirely bad. That must not happen.

There is every degree of distance between the creature and God. A distance where the love of God is impossible. Matter, plants, animals. Here, evil is so complete that it destroys itself: there is no longer any evil: mirror of divine innocence. We are at the point where love is just possible. It is a great privilege, since the love which unites is in proportion to the distance.

God has created a world which is not the best possible, but which contains the whole range of good and evil. We are at the point where it is as bad as possible; for beyond is the stage where evil becomes innocence.

AFFLICTION

Suffering: superiority of man over God. The Incarnation was necessary so that this superiority should not be scandalous.

I should not love my suffering because it is useful. I should love it because it is.

To accept what is bitter. The acceptance must not be reflected back on to the bitterness so as to diminish it, otherwise the acceptance will be proportionately diminished in force and purity, for the thing to be accepted is that which is bitter in so far as it is bitter; it is that and nothing else. We have to say like Ivan Karamazov that nothing can make up for a single tear from a single child, and yet to accept all tears and the nameless horrors which are beyond tears. We have to accept these things, not in so far as they bring compensations with them, but in themselves. We have to accept the fact that they exist simply because they do exist.

If there were no affliction in this world we might think we were in paradise.

Two conceptions of hell: the ordinary one (suffering without consolation); mine (false beatitude, mistakenly thinking oneself to be in paradise).

Greater purity of physical suffering (Thibon). Hence, greater dignity of the people.

We should seek neither to escape suffering nor to suffer less, but to remain untainted by suffering.

The extreme greatness of Christianity lies in the fact that it does not seek a supernatural remedy for suffering but a supernatural use for it.

We should make every effort we can to avoid affliction, so that the affliction which we meet with may be perfectly pure and perfectly bitter.

Joy is the overflowing consciousness of reality.

But to suffer while preserving our consciousness of reality is better. To suffer without being submerged in the nightmare. May the suffering be in one sense purely exterior and in another purely interior. For this to be so it must be situated only in the feelings. Then it is exterior (as it is outside the spiritual part of the soul) and interior (as it is entirely concentrated on ourselves, without being reflected back on to the universe in order to impair it).

Affliction compels us to recognize as real what we do not think possible.

Affliction. Time bears the thinking being in spite of himself towards that which he cannot bear and which will come all the same. 'Let this cup pass from me.' Each second which passes brings some being in the world nearer to something he cannot bear.

There is a point in affliction where we are no longer able to bear either that it should go on or that we should be delivered from it.

Suffering is nothing, apart from the relationship between the past and the future, but what is more real for man than this relationship? It is reality itself.

The future. We go on thinking it will come until the moment when we think it will never come.

Two thoughts lighten affliction a little. Either that it will stop almost immediately or that it will never stop. We can think of it as impossible or necessary, but we can never think that it simply is. That is unendurable.

'It is not possible!' What is not possible is to envisage a future where the affliction will continue. The natural spring of thought towards the future is arrested. We are lacerated in our sense of time. 'In a month, in a year, how shall we suffer?'

The being who can bear to think neither of the past nor the future is reduced to the state of matter. White Russians at Renault's works. Thus one can learn to be obedient like matter, but no doubt they invented for themselves ready-made and illusive pasts and futures.

The fragmentation of time for criminals and prostitutes; it is the same with slaves. This is then a characteristic of affliction.

Time does us violence; it is the only violence. 'Another shall gird thee and lead thee whither thou wouldst not'; time leads us whither we do not wish to go. Were I condemned to death, I should not be executed if, in the interval, time stood still. Whatever frightful thing may happen, can we desire that time should stop, that the stars should be stayed in their courses? Time's violence rends the soul: by the rent eternity enters.

All problems come back again to time. Extreme suffering: undirected time: the way to hell or to paradise. Perpetuity or eternity.

It is not joy and sorrow which are opposed to each other, but the varieties within the one and the other. There are an infernal joy and pain, a healing joy and pain, a celestial joy and pain.

By nature we fly from suffering and seek pleasure. It is for this reason alone that joy serves as an image for good and pain for evil. Hence the imagery of paradise and hell. But as a matter of fact pleasure and pain are inseparable companions.

Suffering, teaching and transformation. What is necessary is not that the initiated should learn something, but that a transformation should come about in them which makes them capable of receiving the teaching.

Pathos means at the same time *suffering* (notably suffering unto death) and *modification* notably transformation into an immortal being).

Suffering and enjoyment as sources of knowledge. The serpent offered knowledge to Adam and Eve. The Sirens offered knowledge to Ulysses. These stories teach that the soul is lost through seeking knowledge in pleasure. Why? Pleasure is perhaps innocent on condition that we do not seek knowledge in it. It is permissible to seek that only in suffering.

The infinite which is in man is at the mercy of a little piece of iron; such is the human condition; space and time are the cause of it. It is impossible to handle this piece of iron without suddenly reducing the infinite which is in man to a point on the pointed part, a point on the handle, at the cost of a harrowing pain. The whole being is stricken on the instant; there is no place left for God, even in the case of Christ, where the thought of God is no more at least than that of privation. This stage has to be reached if there is to be incarnation. The whole being becomes privation of God: how can we go beyond? After that there is only the resurrection. To reach this stage the cold touch of naked iron is necessary.

At the touch of the iron there must be a feeling of separation from God such as Christ experienced, otherwise it is another God. The martyrs did not feel that they were separated from God, but it was another God and it was perhaps better not to be a martyr. The God from whom the martyrs drew joy in torture or death is akin to the one who was officially adopted by the Empire and afterwards imposed by means of exterminations.

To say that the world is not worth anything, that this life is of no value and to give evil as the proof is absurd, for if these things are worthless what does evil take from us?

Thus the better we are able to conceive of the fullness of joy, the purer and more intense will be our suffering in affliction and our compassion for others. What does suffering take from him who is without joy?

And if we conceive the fullness of joy, suffering is still to joy what hunger is to food.

It is necessary to have had a revelation of reality through joy in order to find reality through suffering. Otherwise life is nothing but a more or less evil dream.

We must attain to the knowledge of a still fuller reality in suffering which is a nothingness and a void. In the same way we have greatly to love life in order to love death still more.

VIOLENCE

Death is the most precious thing which has been given to man. That is why the supreme impiety is to make a bad use of it. To die amiss. To kill amiss. (But how can we escape at the same time both from suicide and murder?) After death, love. An analogous problem: neither wrong enjoyment nor wrong privation. War and Eros are the two sources of illusion and falsehood among men. Their mixture represents the very greatest impurity.

We must strive to substitute more and more in this world effective non-violence for violence.

Non-violence is no good unless it is effective. Hence the young man's question to Gandhi about his sister. The answer should have been: use force unless you are such that you can defend her with as much chance of success without violence. Unless you possess a radiance of which the energy (that is to say the possible effectiveness in the most material sense of the word) is equal to that contained in your muscles.

We should strive to become such that we are able to be non-violent.

This depends also on the adversary.

The cause of wars: there is in every man and in every group of men a feeling that they have a just and legitimate claim to be masters of the universe—to possess it. But this possession is not rightly understood because they do not know that each one has access to it (in so far as this is possible for man on this earth) through his own body.

Alexander is to a peasant proprietor what Don Juan is to a happily married husband.

War. To keep the love of life intact within us; never to inflict death without accepting it for ourselves.

Supposing the life of X . . . were linked with our own so that the two deaths had to be simultaneous, should we still wish him to die? If with our whole body and soul we desire life and if nevertheless without lying, we can reply 'yes', then we have the right to kill.

THE CROSS

Whoever takes up the sword shall perish by the sword. And
whoever does not take up the sword (or lets it go) shall perish
on the cross.

Christ healing the sick, raising the dead, etc.—that is the
humble, human, almost low part of his mission. The supernatural part is the sweat of blood, the unsatisfied longing for
human consolation, the supplication that he might be spared,
the sense of being abandoned by God.

The abandonment at the supreme moment of the crucifixion,
what an abyss of love on both sides!

'My God, my God, why has thou forsaken me?'
    There we have the real proof that Christianity is something
divine.

To be just it is necessary to be naked and dead—without

imagination. That is why the model of justice has to be naked and dead. The cross alone is not open to imaginary imitation.

In order that the imitation of God should not be a mere matter of words, it is necessary that there should be a just man to imitate, but in order that we should be carried beyond the will it is necessary that we should not be able to choose to imitate him. One cannot choose the cross.

One might choose no matter what degree of asceticism or heroism, but not the cross, that is to say penal suffering.

Those who can only conceive of the crucifixion under the aspect of an offering do away with the salutary mystery and the salutary bitterness of it. To wish for martyrdom is far too little. The cross is infinitely more than martyrdom.

It is the most purely bitter suffering—penal suffering. This is the guarantee of its authenticity.

The cross. The tree of sin was a real tree, the tree of life was a wooden beam. Something which does not give fruit, but only vertical movement. 'The Son of Man must be lifted up and he will draw all men unto himself.' We can kill the vital energy in ourselves while keeping only the vertical movement. Leaves and fruit are a waste of energy if our only wish is to rise.

Adam and Eve sought for divinity in vital energy—a tree, fruit. But it is prepared for us on dead wood, geometrically squared, where a corpse is hanging. We must look for the secret of our kinship with God in our mortality.

God wears himself out through the infinite thickness of time and space in order to reach the soul and to captivate it. If it allows a pure and utter consent (though brief as a lightning flash) to be torn from it, then God conquers that soul. And when it has become entirely his he abandons it. He leaves it completely alone and it has in its turn, but gropingly, to cross the infinite thickness of time and space in search of him whom it loves. It is thus that the soul, starting from the opposite end, makes the same journey that God made towards it. And that is the cross.

God is crucified from the fact that finite beings, subject to necessity, to space and to time, think.

I have to know that as a thinking, finite being I am God crucified.

I have to be like God, but like God crucified.

Like God almighty in so far as he is bound by necessity.

Prometheus—the god crucified for having loved men too much. Hippolytus, the man punished for having been too pure and too much loved by the gods. It is the coming together of the human and the divine which calls forth punishment.

We are what is furthest from God, situated at the extreme limit from which it is not absolutely impossible to come back to him. In our being, God is torn. We are the crucifixion of God. The love of God for us is a passion. How could that which is good love that which is evil without suffering? And that which is evil suffers too in loving that which is good. The mutual love of God and man is suffering.

In order that we should realize the distance between ourselves and God it was necessary that God should be a crucified slave. For we do not realize distance except in the downward direction. It is much easier to imagine ourselves in the place of God the Creator than in the place of Christ crucified.

The dimensions of Christ's charity are the same as the distance between God and the creature.

The function of mediation in itself implies a tearing asunder.

That is why we cannot conceive of the descent of God towards men or the ascent of man towards God without a tearing asunder.

We have to cross the infinite thickness of time and space—and God has to do it first, because he comes to us first. Of the links between God and man, love is the greatest. It is as great as the distance to be crossed.

So that the love may be as great as possible, the distance is as great as possible. That is why evil can extend to the extreme limit beyond which the very possibility of good disappears. Evil is permitted to touch this limit. It sometimes seems as though it overpassed it.

This, in a sense, is exactly the opposite of what Leibniz thought. It is certainly more compatible with God's greatness, for if he had made the best of all possible worlds, it would mean that he could not do very much.

God crosses through the thickness of the world to come to us.

The Passion is the existence of perfect justice without any admixture of appearance. Justice is essentially non-active. It must either be transcendent or suffering.

The Passion is purely supernatural justice, absolutely stripped of all sensible help, even of the love of God in so far as it can be felt.

Redemptive suffering is that which strips suffering naked and brings it in its purity right into existence. That saves existence.

As God is present through the consecration of the Eucharist in what the senses perceive as a morsel of bread, so he is present in extreme evil through redemptive suffering through the cross.

From human misery to God. But not as a compensation or consolation. As a correlation.

There are people for whom everything is salutary which brings God nearer to them. For me it is everything which keeps him at a distance. Between me and him there is the thickness of the universe—and that of the cross is added to it.

Suffering is at the same time quite external with regard to innocence and quite essential to it.

Blood on snow. Innocence and evil. Evil itself must be pure. It can only be pure in the form of the suffering of someone innocent. An innocent being who suffers sheds the light of salvation upon evil. Such a one is the visible image of the innocent God. That is why a God who loves man and a man who loves God have to suffer.

Happy innocence. That also is something precious. But it is a precarious and fragile happiness, a happiness which depends on chance. The blossom of apple trees. Happiness is not bound up with innocence.

To be innocent is to bear the weight of the entire universe. It is to throw away the counterweight.

In emptying ourselves we expose ourselves to all the pressure of the surrounding universe.

God gives himself to men either as powerful or as perfect—it is for them to choose.

BALANCE AND LEVER

The cross as a balance, as a lever. A going down, the condition of a rising up. Heaven coming down to earth raises earth to heaven.

A lever. We lower when we want to lift.

In the same way 'he who humbleth himself shall be exalted'.

There are necessity and laws in the realm of grace likewise. Even hell has its laws (Goethe). So has heaven.

A strict necessity which excludes all that is arbitrary or dependent on chance rules over mathematical phenomena. Although they are free, there is if possible even less arbitrariness and chance in spiritual matters.

One—the smallest of the numbers.

'The One that alone is wise.' That is the infinite. A number which increases thinks that it is getting near to infinity. It is receding from it. We must stoop in order to rise.

If 1 is God, ∞ is the devil.

It is human misery and not pleasure which contains the secret of the divine wisdom. All pleasure-seeking is the search for an artificial paradise, an intoxication, an enlargement. But it gives us nothing except the experience that it is vain. Only the contemplation of our limitations and our misery puts us on a higher plane. 'Whosoever humbleth himself shall be exalted.'

The upward movement in us is vain (and less than vain) if it does not come from a downward movement.

Statera facta corporis. It is the crucified body which is a true balance, the body reduced to its point in time and space.

We must not judge. We must be like the Father in heaven who does not judge: by him beings judge themselves. We must let all beings come to us, and leave them to judge themselves. We must be a balance.

Then we shall not be judged, having become an image of the true judge who does not judge.

When the whole universe weighs upon us there is no other counterweight possible but God himself—the true God, for in this case false gods cannot do anything, not even under the name of the true one. Evil is infinite in the sense of being indefinite: matter, space, time. Nothing can overcome this kind of infinity except the true infinity. That is why on the balance of the cross a body which was frail and light but which was God, lifted up the whole world. 'Give me a point of leverage and I will lift up the world.' This point of leverage is the cross. There can be no other. It has to be at the intersection of the world and that which is not the world. The cross is this intersection.

THE IMPOSSIBLE

Human life is impossible. But it is only affliction which makes us feel this.

The impossibility of good: 'Good comes out of evil, evil out of good, and when will it all end?'

The good is impossible. But man always has enough imagination at his disposal to hide from himself in each particular case the impossibility of good (it is enough if for each event which does not crush us ourselves we can veil part of the evil and add a fictitous good—and some people manage to do this even if they are crushed themselves). Man's imagination at the same time prevents him from seeing 'how much the essence of the necessary differs from that of the good,' and prevents him from allowing himself really to meet God who is none other than the good itself—the good which is found nowhere in this world.

Desire is impossible: it destroys its object. Lovers cannot be one, nor can Narcissus be two. Don Juan, Narcissus. Because to desire something is impossible, we have to desire what is nothing.

Our life is impossibility, absurdity. Everything we want contradicts the conditions or the consequences attached to it, every affirmation we put forward involves a contradictory affirmation, all our feelings are mixed up with their opposites. It is because we are a contradiction—being creatures—being God and infinitely other than God.

Contradiction alone is the proof that we are not everything. Contradiction is our wretchedness, and the sense of our wretchedness is the sense of reality. For we do not invent our wretchedness. It is true. That is why we have to value it. All the rest is imaginary.

Impossibility is the door of the supernatural. We can but knock at it. It is someone else who opens.

It is necessary to touch impossibility in order to come out of the dream world. There is no impossibility in dreams—only impotence.

'Our Father, he who is in heaven.' There is a sort of humour in that. He is your Father, but just try to go and look for him up there! We are quite as incapable of rising from the ground as an earth-worm. And how should he for his part come to us without descending? There is no way of imagining a contact between God and man which is not as unintelligible as the incarnation. The incarnation explodes this unintelligibility. It is the most concrete way of representing this impossible descent. Hence why should it not be the truth?

The links that we cannot forge are evidence of the transcendent.

We are beings with the faculty of knowing, willing and loving, and as soon as we turn our attention towards the objects of knowledge, will and love, we receive evidence that there is not one which is not *impossible*. Falsehood alone can veil such evidence. Consciousness of this impossibility forces us to long continually to grasp what cannot be grasped in all that we desire, know and will.

When something seems impossible to obtain despite every effort, it is an indication of a limit which cannot be passed on that plane and of the necessity for a change of level—a break in the ceiling. To wear ourselves out in efforts on the same level degrades us. It is better to accept the limit, to contemplate it and savour all its bitterness.

Error as an incentive, a source of energy. I think I see a friend. I run towards him. When I come a little nearer I see that it is someone else towards whom I am running—a stranger. In the same way we confuse the relative with the absolute—created things with God.

All particular incentives are errors. Only that energy which is not due to any incentive is good: obedience to God, which, since God is beyond all that we can imagine or conceive, means obedience to nothing. This is at the same time impossible and necessary—in other words it is supernatural.

A benefit (*bienfait*). A good action is such if in doing it we realise with our *whole* soul that such a thing as a benefit is absolutely impossible.

To do good. Whatever I do I know perfectly clearly that it is not good, for he who is not good cannot do good. And 'God alone is good . . .'

On every occasion, whatever we do, we do evil, and an intolerable evil.

We must ask that all the evil we do may fall solely and directly on ourselves. That is the cross.

That action is good which we are able to accomplish while keeping our attention and intention totally directed towards pure and impossible goodness, without veiling from ourselves by any falsehood either the attraction or the impossibility of pure goodness.

In this way virtue is entirely analogous to artistic inspiration. The beautiful poem is the one which is composed while the attention is kept directed towards inexpressible inspiration, in so far as it is inexpressible.

CONTRADICTION

The contradictions the mind comes up against—these are the only realities: they are the criterion of the real. There is no contradiction in what is imaginary. Contradiction is the test of necessity.

Contradiction experienced to the very depths of the being tears us heart and soul: it is the cross.

When the attention has revealed the contradiction in something on which it has been fixed, a kind of loosening takes place. By persevering in this course we attain detachment.

The demonstrable correlation of opposites is an image of the transcendental correlation of contradictories.

All true good carries with it conditions which are contradictory and as a consequence is impossible. He who keeps his attention really fixed on this impossibility and acts will do what is good.

In the same way all truth contains a contradiction.

Contradiction is the point of the pyramid.

The word good has not the same meaning when it is a term of the correlation good-evil as when it describes the very being of God.

The existence of opposite virtues in the souls of the saints: the metaphor of climbing corresponds to this. If I am walking on the side of a mountain I can see first a lake, then, after a few steps, a forest. I have to choose either the lake or the forest. If I want to see both lake and forest at once, I have to climb higher.

Only the mountain does not exist. It is made of air. One cannot go up: it is necessary to be drawn.

An experimental ontological proof. I have not the principle of rising in me. I cannot climb to heaven through the air. It is only by directing my thoughts towards something better than myself that I am drawn upwards by this something. If I am really raised up, this something is real. No imaginary perfection can draw me upwards even by the fraction of an inch. For an imaginary perfection is automatically at the same level as I who imagine it—neither higher nor lower.

What is thus brought about by thought direction is in no way comparable to suggestion. If I say to myself every morning: 'I am courageous, I am not afraid', I may become courageous but with a courage which conforms to what, in my present imperfection, I imagine under that name, and accordingly my courage will not go beyond this imperfection. It can only be a modification on the same plane, not a change of plane.

Contradiction is the criterion. We cannot by suggestion obtain things which are incompatible. Only grace can do that. A sensitive person who by suggestion becomes courageous hardens himself; often he may even, by a sort of savage pleasure, amputate his own sensitivity. Grace alone can give courage while leaving the sensitivity intact, or sensitivity while leaving the courage intact.

Man's great affliction, which begins with infancy and accompanies him till death, is that looking and eating are two different operations. Eternal beatitude is a state where to look is to eat.

That which we look at here below is not real, it is a mere setting. That which we eat is destroyed, it is no longer real.

Sin has brought this separation about in us.

The natural virtues, if we give the word virtue its authentic meaning, that is to say if we exclude the social imitations of virtue, are only possible as permanent attributes for someone who has supernatural grace within him. Their duration is supernatural.

Opposites and contradictories. What the relation of opposites can do in the approach to the natural being, the unifying grasp of contradictory ideas can do in the approach to God.

A man inspired by God is a man who has ways of behaviour, thoughts and feelings which are bound together by a bond impossible to define.

Pythagorean idea: the good is always defined by the union of opposites. When we recommend the opposite of an evil we remain on the level of that evil. After we have put it to the test, we return to the evil. That is what the Gita calls 'the aberration of opposites'. Marxist dialectic is based on a very degraded and completely warped view of this.

A wrong union of contraries. The imperialism of the working class developed by Marxism. Latin proverbs concerning the insolence of newly-freed slaves. Insolence and servility are aggravated by each other. Sincere anarchists, discerning, as through a mist, the principle of the union of opposites, thought that evil could be destroyed by giving power to the oppressed. An impossible dream.

What then differentiates the right from the wrong union of opposites.

Bad union of opposites (bad because fallacious) is that which is achieved on the same plane as the opposites. Thus the granting of domination to the oppressed. In this way we do not get free from the oppression-domination cycle.

The right union of opposites is achieved on a higher plane. Thus the opposition between domination and oppression is smoothed out on the level of the law—which is balance.

In the same way suffering (and this is its special function) separates the opposites which have been united in order to unite them again on a higher plane than that of their first union. The pulsation of sorrow-joy. But, mathematically, joy always triumphs.

Suffering is violence, joy is gentleness, but joy is the stronger.

The union of contradictories involves a wrenching apart. It is impossible without extreme suffering.

The correlation of contradictories is detachment. An attachment to a particular thing can only be destroyed by an attachment which is incompatible with it. That explains: 'Love your enemies. . . . He who hateth not his father and mother . . .'

Either we have made the contraries submissive to us or we have submitted to the contraries.

Simultaneous existence of incompatible things in the soul's bearing; balance which leans both ways at once: that is saintliness, the actual realization of the microcosm, the imitation of the order of the world.

The simultaneous existence of opposite virtues in the soul—like pincers to catch hold of God.

We have to find out and formulate certain general laws relating to man's condition, concerning which many profound observations throw light on particular cases.

Thus: that which is in every way superior reproduces that which is in every way inferior, but transposed.

Relationships of evil to strength and to being; and of good to weakness or nothingness.

Yet at the same time evil is privation. We have to elucidate the way contradictories have of being true.

Method of investigation: as soon as we have thought something, try to see in what way the contrary is true.[1]

Evil is the shadow of good. All real good, possessing solidity and thickness, projects evil. Only imaginary good does not project it.

As all good is attached to evil, if we desire the good and do not wish to spread the corresponding evil round us we are obliged, since we cannot avoid this evil, to concentrate it on ourselves.

Thus the desire for utterly pure good involves the acceptance of the last degree of affliction for ourselves.

If we desire nothing but good, we are opposing the law which links real good to evil as the object in the light is linked to its

---

[1] This aphorism gives us the key to the *apparent* contradictions scattered throughout the work of Simone Weil: love of tradition and detachment from the past, God conceived of as the supreme reality and as nothingness, etc. These contradictory ideas are true on different planes of existence and their opposition is smoothed out on the level of supernatural love. Reason discerns the two ends of the chain but the centre which unites them is only accessible to undemonstrable intuition.   [Editor's note.]

shadow, and, being opposed to one of the world's universal laws, it is inevitable that we should fall into affliction.

The mystery of the cross of Christ lies in a contradiction, for it is both a free-will offering and a punishment which he endured in spite of himself. If we only saw in it an offering, we might wish for a like fate. But we are unable to wish for a punishment endured in spite of ourselves.

THE DISTANCE BETWEEN THE NECESSARY AND THE GOOD[1]

Necessity is God's veil.

God has committed all phenomena without exception to the mechanism of the world.[2]

As there is in God the analogy of every human virtue, so there is obedience. This is the free play he allows necessity in this world.

---

[1] Cf. Plato, *Republic*, Book VI.   [Editor's note.]

[2] It is significant to notice that Simone Weil extends the determinism of Descartes and Spinoza to *all natural* phenomena, including the facts of psychology. Gravity for her is only held in check by grace. She thus overlooks the margin of indetermination and spontaneity which God has left in nature and which allows for the introduction of liberty and miracles in the world. It remains none the less true that *in fact* gravity is practically all-powerfitl: Saint Thomas recognizes that most human actions are prompted by the blind appetite of the senses and subject to the determination of the stars.   [Editor's note.]

Necessity—an image by which the mind can conceive of the indifference, the impartiality of God.

Thus the ordinary notion of miracles is a kind of impiety (a miracle being thought of as something which has no secondary cause but only a first cause).

The distance between the necessary and the good is the distance between the creature and the creator.

The distance between the necessary and the good: this is a subject for endless contemplation. It was the great discovery of Greece. No doubt the fall of Troy taught it them.

Every attempt to justify evil by anything other than the fact that that which is is, is an offence against this truth.

We aspire only to get rid of the intolerable burden of the good-evil cycle—a burden assumed by Adam and Eve.

In order to do that it is necessary either to confuse 'the essence of the necessary with that of the good' or to depart from this world.

Evil can only be purified by God or by the Social Beast. Purity purifies evil—so does force in quite another way. In the case of one who is able to do all things, all things are permitted. He who serves an all-powerful master can do all things through him. Force delivers us from the good-evil cycle. It delivers him who exercises it and even him also who submits to it. A master has every licence, so has a slave. The sword affords deliverance (whether through its handle or its point) from the intolerable weight of our obligation. Grace also delivers us from the burden but we only go towards it through obligation.

We only escape limitation by rising up towards unity or going down towards the limitless.

Limitation is the evidence that God loves us.

The idea that the end of the world was near, coloured the outlook of the early Christians. This belief produced in them a 'forgetfulness of the immense distance which divides the necessary from the good.'

The absence of God is the most marvellous testimony of perfect love, and that is why pure necessity, necessity which is manifestly different from good, is so beautiful.

The limitless is the test of the one: time, of eternity: the possible, of necessity: variety, of the unvarying.

The value of a system of knowledge, a work of art, a moral code or a soul is measured by the degree of its resistance to this test.

CHANCE

The beings I love are creatures. They were born by chance. My meeting with them was also by chance. They will die. What they think, do and say is limited and is a mixture of good and evil.

I have to know this with all my soul and not love them the less.

I have to imitate God who infinitely loves finite things in that they are finite things.

We want everything which has a value to be eternal. Now everything which has a value is the product of a meeting, lasts throughout this meeting and ceases when those things which met are separated. That is the central idea of Buddhism (the thought of Heraclitus). It leads straight to God.

Meditation on chance which led to the meeting of my father and mother is even more salutary than meditation on death.

Is there a single thing in me of which the origin is not to be

found in that meeting? Only God. And yet again, my thought of
God had its origin in that meeting.

Stars and blossoming fruit-trees: utter permanence and extreme
fragility give an equal sense of eternity.

The theories about progress and the 'genius which always
pierces through', arise from the fact that it is intolerable to suppose that what is most precious in the world should be given
over to chance. It is because it is intolerable that it ought to be
contemplated.

Creation is this very thing.

The only good which is not subject to chance is that which is
outside the world.

The vulnerability of precious things is beautiful because
vulnerability is a mark of existence.

The destruction of Troy. The fall of the petals from fruit trees
in blossom. To know that what is most precious is not rooted in
existence—that is beautiful. Why? It projects the soul beyond
time.

The woman who wishes for a child white as snow and red as
blood gets it, but she dies and the child is given over to a
stepmother.

HE WHOM WE MUST LOVE
IS ABSENT

God can only be present in creation under the form of absence.

Evil is the innocence of God. We have to place God at an infinite distance in order to conceive of him as innocent of evil; reciprocally, evil implies that we have to place God at an infinite distance.

This world, in so far as it is completely empty of God, is God himself.

Necessity, in so far as it is absolutely other than the good, is the good itself.

That is why all consolation in affliction separates us from love and from truth.

That is the mystery of mysteries. When we touch it we are safe.

'In the desert of the East. . . .' We have to be in a desert. For he whom we must love is absent.

He who puts his life into his faith in God can loose his faith.

But he who puts his life in God himself will never lose it. To put our life into that which we cannot touch in any way. . . . It is impossible. It is a death. That is what is required.

Nothing which exists is absolutely worthy of love.

We must therefore love that which does not exist.

This non-existent object of love is not a fiction, however, for our fictions cannot be any more worthy of love than we are ourselves, and we are not worthy of it.

Consent to the good—not to any good which can be grasped or represented, but unconditional consent to the absolute good.

When we consent to something which we represent to ourselves as the good, we consent to a mixture of good and evil, and this consent produces good and evil: the proportion of good and evil in us does not change. On the other hand the unconditional consent to that good which we are not able and never will be able to represent to ourselves—such consent is pure good and produces only good, moreover, it is enough that it should continue for the whole soul to be nothing but good in the end.

Faith (when it is a question of a supernatural interpretation of the natural) is a conjecture by analogy based on supernatural experience. Thus those who have the privilege of mystical contemplation, having experienced the mercy of God, *suppose* that, God being mercy, the created world is a work of mercy. But as for obtaining evidence of this mercy directly from nature, it would be necessary to become blind, deaf and without pity in order to believe such a thing possible. Thus the Jews and Moslems, who want to find in nature the proofs of divine mercy, are pitiless. And often the Christians are as well.

That is why mysticism is the only source of virtue for humanity. Because when men do not believe that there is infinite mercy behind the curtain of the world, or when they think that this mercy is in front of the curtain, they become cruel.

There are four evidences of divine mercy here below: the favours of God to beings capable of contemplation (these states exist and form part of their experience as creatures); the radiance of these beings and their compassion, which is the divine compassion in them; the beauty of the world. The fourth evidence is the complete absence of mercy here below.[1]

Incarnation. God is weak because he is impartial. He sends sunshine and rain to good and evil alike. This indifference of the Father and the weakness of Christ correspond. Absence of God. The kingdom of heaven is like a grain of mustard seed. . . . God changes nothing whatsoever. Christ was killed out of anger because he was only God.

If I thought that God sent me suffering by an act of his will and for my good, I should think that I was something, and I should miss the chief use of suffering which is to teach me that I am nothing. It is therefore essential to avoid all such thoughts, but it is necessary to love God through the suffering.

I must love being nothing. How horrible it would be if I were something! I must love my nothingness, love being a nothingness. I must love with that part of the soul which is on the other side of the curtain, for the part of the soul which is perceptible to consciousness cannot love nothingness. It has a horror of it. Though it may think it loves nothingness, what it really loves is something other than nothingness.

---

[1] It is precisely by this antithesis, this rending of our souls between the effects of grace within us and the beauty of the world around us, on the one hand, and the implacable necessity which rules the universe on the other, that we discern God as both present to man and as absolutely beyond all human measurement.

God sends affliction without distinction to the wicked and to the good, just as he sends the rain and the sunlight. He did not reserve the cross for Christ. He enters into contact with a human individual as such only through purely spiritual grace which responds to the gaze turned towards him, that is to say to the exact extent to which the individual ceases to be an individual. No event is a favour on the part of God—only grace is that.

Communion is good for the good and bad for the wicked. Hence, damned souls are in paradise, but for them paradise is hell.

The cry of suffering: 'Why?' This rings throughout the Iliad.

To explain suffering is to console it; therefore it must not be explained.

Herein lies the pre-eminent value of the suffering of those who are innocent. It bears a resemblance to the acceptance of the evil in creation by God who is innocent.

The irreducible character of suffering which makes it impossible for us not to have a horror of it at the moment when we are undergoing it is destined to bring the will to a standstill, just as absurdity brings the intelligence to a standstill, and absence love, so that man, having come to the end of his human faculties, may stretch out his arms, stop, look up and wait.

'He will laugh at the trials of the innocent.' Silence of God. The noises here below imitate this silence. They mean nothing.

It is when from the innermost depths of our being we need a sound which does mean something—when we cry out for an answer and it is not given us—it is then that we touch the silence of God.

As a rule our imagination puts words into the sounds in the same way as we idly play at making out shapes in wreaths of smoke; but when we are too exhausted, when we no longer have the courage to play, then we must have real words. We cry out for them. The cry tears our very entrails. All we get is silence.

After having gone through that, some begin to talk to themselves like madmen. Whatever they may do afterwards, we must have nothing but pity for them. The others, and they are not numerous, give their whole heart to silence.

ATHEISM AS A
PURIFICATION

A case of contradictories which are true. God exists: God does not exist. Where is the problem? I am quite sure that there is a God in the sense that I am quite sure my love is not illusory. I am quite sure that there is not a God in the sense that I am quite sure nothing real can be anything like what I am able to conceive when I pronounce this word. But that which I cannot conceive is not an illusion.

There are two atheisms of which one is a purification of the notion of God.

Perhaps every evil thing has a second aspect—a purification in the course of progress towards the good—and a third which is the higher good.

We have to distinguish carefully between these three aspects because it is very dangerous for thought and for the effective conduct of life to confuse them.

Of two men who have no experience of God, he who denies him is perhaps nearer to him than the other.

The false God who is like the true one in everything, except that we cannot touch him, prevents us from ever coming to the true one.

We have to believe in a God who is like the true God in everything, except that he does not exist, since we have not reached the point where God exists.

The errors of our time come from Christianity without the supernatural. Secularization is the cause—and primarily humanism.

Religion in so far as it is a source of consolation is a hindrance to true faith: in this sense atheism is a purification. I have to be atheistic with the part of myself which is not made for God. Among those men in whom the supernatural part has not been awakened, the atheists are right and the believers wrong.

A man whose whole family had died under torture, and who had himself been tortured for a long time in a concentration camp; or a sixteenth-century Indian, the sole survivor after the total extermination of his people. Such men if they had previously believed in the mercy of God would either believe in it no longer, or else they would conceive of it quite differently from before. I have not been through such things. I know, however, that they exist; so what is the difference?

I must move towards an abiding conception of the divine mercy, a conception which does not change whatever event destiny may send upon me and which can be communicated to no matter what human being.

ATTENTION AND WILL

We do not have to understand new things, but by dint of patience, effort and method to come to understand with our whole self the truths which are evident.

Stages of belief. The most commonplace truth when it floods the whole soul, is like a revelation.

We have to try to cure our faults by attention and not by will.
    The will only controls a few movements of a few muscles, and these movements are associated with the idea of the change of position of near-by objects. I can will to put my hand flat on the table. If inner purity, inspiration or truth of thought were necessarily associated with attitudes of this kind, they might be the object of will. As this is not the case, we can only beg for them. To beg for them is to believe that we have a Father in heaven. Or should we cease to desire them? What could be worse? Inner supplication is the only reasonable way, for it avoids stiffening muscles which have nothing to do with the matter. What could

be more stupid than to tighten up our muscles and set our jaws about virtue, or poetry, or the solution of a problem. Attention is something quite different.

Pride is a tightening up of this kind. There is a lack of grace (we can give the word its double meaning here) in the proud man. It is the result of a mistake.

Attention, taken to its highest degree, is the same thing as prayer. It presupposes faith and love.

Absolutely unmixed attention is prayer.

If we turn our mind towards the good, it is impossible that little by little the whole soul will not be attracted thereto in spite of itself.

Extreme attention is what constitutes the creative faculty in man and the only extreme attention is religious. The amount of creative genius in any period is strictly in proportion to the amount of extreme attention and thus of authentic religion at that period.

The wrong way of seeking. The attention fixed on a problem. Another phenomenon due to horror of the void. We do not want to have lost our labour. The heat of the chase. We must not want to find: as in the case of an excessive devotion, we become dependent on the object of our efforts. We need an outward reward which chance sometimes provides and which we are ready to accept at the price of a deformation of the truth.

It is only effort without desire (not attached to an object) which infallibly contains a reward.

To draw back before the object we are pursuing. Only an indirect method is effective. We do nothing if we have not first drawn back.

By pulling at the bunch, we make all the grapes fall to the ground.

There are some kinds of effort which defeat their own object (example: the soured disposition of certain pious females, false asceticism, certain sorts of self-devotion, etc.). Others are always useful, even if they do not meet with success.

How are we to distinguish between them?

Perhaps in this way: some efforts are always accompanied by the (false) negation of our inner wretchedness; with others the attention is continually concentrated on the distance there is between what we are and what we love.

Love is the teacher of gods and men, for no one learns without desiring to learn. Truth is sought not because it is truth but because it is good.

Attention is bound up with desire. Not with the will but with desire—or more exactly, consent.

We liberate energy in ourselves, but it constantly reattaches itself. How are we to liberate it entirely? We have to desire that it should be done in us—to desire it truly—simply to desire it, not to try to accomplish it. For every attempt in that direction is vain and has to be dearly paid for. In such a work all that I call 'I' has to be passive. Attention alone—that attention which is so full that the 'I' disappears—is required of me. I have to deprive all that I call 'I' of the light of my attention and turn it on to that which cannot be conceived.

The capacity to drive a thought away once and for all is the gateway to eternity. The infinite in an instant.

As regards temptations, we must follow the example of the truly chaste woman who, when the seducer speaks to her, makes no answer and pretends not to hear him.

We should be indifferent to good and evil but, when we are indifferent, that is to say when we project the light of our attention equally on both, the good gains the day. This phenomenon comes about automatically. There lies the essential grace. And it is the definition, the criterion of good.

A divine inspiration operates infallibly, irresistibly, if we do not turn away our attention, if we do not refuse it. There is not a choice to be made in its favour, it is enough not to refuse to recognize that it exists.

The attention turned with love towards God (or in a lesser degree, towards anything which is truly beautiful) makes certain things impossible for us. Such is the non-acting action of prayer in the soul. There are ways of behaviour which would veil such attention should they be indulged in and which, reciprocally, this attention puts out of the question.

As soon as we have a point of eternity in the soul, we have nothing more to do but to take care of it, for it will grow of itself like a seed. It is necessary to surround it with an armed guard, waiting in stillness, and to nourish it with the contemplation of numbers, of fixed and exact relationships.

We nourish the changeless which is in the soul by the contemplation of that which is unchanging in the body.

Writing is like giving birth: we cannot help making the supreme effort. But we also act in like fashion. I need have no fear of not making the supreme effort—provided only that I am honest with myself and that I pay attention.

The poet produces the beautiful by fixing his attention on something real. It is the same with the act of love. To know that this man who is hungry and thirsty really exists as much as I do— that is enough, the rest follows of itself.

The authentic and pure values—truth, beauty and goodness—in the activity of a human being are the result of one and the same act, a certain application of the full attention to the object.

Teaching should have no aim but to prepare, by training the attention, for the possibility of such an act.

All the other advantages of instruction are without interest.

Studies and faith. Prayer being only attention in its pure form and studies being a form of gymnastics of the attention, each school exercise should be a refraction of spiritual life. There must be method in it. A certain way of doing a Latin prose, a certain way of tackling a problem in geometry (and not just any way) make up a system of gymnastics of the attention calculated to give it a greater aptitude for prayer.

Method for understanding images, symbols, etc. Not to try to interpret them, but to look at them till the light suddenly dawns.

Generally speaking, a method for the exercise of the intelligence, which consists of looking.

Application of this rule for the discrimination between the real and the illusory. In our sense perceptions, if we are not sure of what we see we change our position while looking, and what is real becomes evident. In the inner life, time takes the place of space. With time we are altered, and, if as we change we keep our gaze directed towards the same thing, in the end illusions are scattered and the real becomes visible. This is on condition that the attention be a looking and not an attachment.

When a struggle goes on between the will attached to some obligation and a bad desire, there is a wearing away of the energy attached to good. We have to endure the biting of the desire passively, as we do a suffering which brings home to us our wretchedness, and we have to keep our attention turned towards the good. Then the quality of our energy is raised to a higher degree.

We must steal away the energy from our desires by taking away from them their temporal orientation.

Our desires are infinite in their pretensions but limited by the energy from which they proceed. That is why with the help of grace we can become their master and finally destroy them by attrition. As soon as this has been clearly understood, we have virtually conquered them, if we keep our attention in contact with this truth.

Video meliora . . . In such states, it seems as though we were thinking of the good, and in a sense we are doing so, but we are not thinking of its possibility.

It is incontestable that the void which we grasp with the pincers of contradiction is from on high, for we grasp it the better the more we sharpen our natural faculties of intelligence, will and love. The void which is from below is that into which we fall when we allow our natural faculties to become atrophied.

Experience of the transcendent: this seems contradictory, and yet the transcendent can be known only through contact since our faculties are unable to invent it.

Solitude. Where does its value lie? For in solitude we are in the presence of mere matter (even the sky, the stars, the moon, trees in blossom), things of less value (perhaps) than a human spirit. Its value lies in the greater possibility of attention. If we could be attentive to the same degree in the presence of a human being . . .

We can only know one thing about God—that he is what we are

not. Our wretchedness alone is an image of this. The more we contemplate it, the more we contemplate him.

Sin is nothing else but the failure to recognize human wretchedness. It is unconscious wretchedness and for that very reason guilty wretchedness. The story of Christ is the experimental proof that human wretchedness is irreducible, that it is as great in the absolutely sinless man as in the sinner. But in him who is without sin it is enlightened . . .

The recognition of human wretchedness is difficult for whoever is rich and powerful because he is almost invincibly led to believe that he is something. It is equally difficult for the man in miserable circumstances because he is almost invincibly led to believe that the rich and powerful man is something.

It is not the fault which constitutes mortal sin, but the degree of light in the soul when the fault, whatever it may be, is accomplished.

Purity is the power to contemplate defilement.

Extreme purity can contemplate both the pure and the impure; impurity can do neither: the pure frightens it, the impure absorbs it. It has to have a mixture.

TRAINING

We have to accomplish the possible in order to touch the impossible. The correct exercise (according to our duty) of the natural faculties of will, love and knowledge is, in relation to spiritual realities, exactly what the movement of the body is in relation to the perception of tangible objects. A paralyzed man lacks this perception.

The fulfilment of our strictly human duty is of the same order as correctness in the work of drafting, translating, calculating, etc. To be careless about this correctness shows a lack of respect for the object. The same thing applies to neglect of duty.

Those things which have to do with inspiration are the only ones which are the better for delay. Those which have to do with natural duty and the will cannot allow of delay.

Precepts are not given for the sake of being practised, but practice is prescribed in order that precepts may be understood. They are scales. One does not play Bach without having done scales. But neither does one play a scale merely for the sake of the scale.

Training. Every time we catch ourselves involuntarily indulging in a proud thought, we must for a few seconds turn the full gaze of our attention upon the memory of some humiliation in our past life, choosing the most bitter, the most intolerable we can think of.

We must not try to change within ourselves or to efface desires and aversions, pleasures and sorrows. We must submit to them passively, just as we do to the impressions we receive from colours, according no greater credit to them than in the latter case. If my window is red I cannot, though I should reason day and night for a whole year, see my room as anything but pink. I know, moreover, that it is necessary, just and right that I should see it thus. At the same time, as far as information about my room goes, I only accord to the pink colour a credit limited by my knowledge of its relation to the window. I must accept in this way and no other the desires and aversions, pleasures and sorrows of every kind which I find within me.

On the other hand, as we have also a principle of violence in us—that is to say the will—we must also, in a limited measure, but to the full extent of that measure, use this violent principle in a violent way; we must compel ourselves by violence to act as though we had not a certain desire or aversion, without trying to persuade our sensibility—compelling it to obey. This causes it to revolt and we have to endure this revolt passively, taste of it, savour it, accept it as something outside ourselves, as the pink colour of the room with the red window.

Each time that we do violence to ourselves in this spirit we make an advance, slight or great but real, in the work of training the animal within us.

Of course if this violence we do ourselves is really to be of use in our training it must only be a means. When a man trains a dog to perform tricks he does not beat it for the sake of beating it, but in order to train it, and with this in view he only hits it when it fails to carry out a trick. If he beats it without any method he ends by making it unfit for any training, and that is what the wrong sort of asceticism does.

Violence against ourselves is only permissible when it is based on reason (with a view to carrying out what we clearly consider to be our duty)—or when it is enjoined on us through an irresistible impulsion on the part of grace (but then the violence does not come from ourselves).

The source of my difficulties lies in the fact that, through exhaustion and an absence of vital energy, I am below the level of normal activity. And if something takes me and raises me up I am lifted above it. When such moments come it would seem to me a calamity to waste them in ordinary activities. At other times, I should have to do violence to myself with a violence which I cannot succeed in mustering.

I could consent to the anomaly of behaviour resulting from this; but I know, or I believe I know, that I should not do so. It involves crimes of omission towards others. And as for myself, it imprisons me.

What method is there then?

ἐὰν θέλῃς δύνασαι μὲ καθαρίσαι[1]

I must practise transforming the sense of effort into a passive sense of suffering. Whatever I may have to bear, when God sends me suffering, I am inescapably forced to suffer all that there is to suffer. Why, when it comes to duty, should I not in like manner do all that there is to be done?

---

[1] 'If thou wilt thou canst make me clean' (Gospel text).

Mountains, rocks, fall upon us and hide us far from the wrath of the Lamb.

At the present moment I deserve this wrath.

I must not forget that according to Saint John of the Cross the inspirations which turn us from the accomplishment of easy and humble obligations come from the side of evil.

Duty is given us in order to kill the self—and I allow so precious an instrument to grow rusty.

We must do our duty at the prescribed time in order to believe in the reality of the external world. We must believe in the reality of time. Otherwise we are in a dream.

It is years since I recognized this defect in myself and recognized its importance, and all this time I have done nothing to get rid of it. What excuse can I find?

Has it not been growing in me since I was ten years old? But however great it may be, it is limited. That is enough. If it is great enough to take from me the possibility of wiping it out during this life and so attaining to the state of perfection, that must be accepted just as it is, with an acceptance that is full of love. It is enough that I know that it exists, that it is evil and that it is finite. But to know each of these three things effectively and to know them all three together implies the beginning and the uninterrupted continuation of the process of wiping out. If this process does not begin to show itself, it is a sign that I do not know in truth the very thing that I am writing.

The necessary energy dwells in me, since I live by means of it. I must draw it relentlessly out of myself, even though I should die in so doing.

Uninterrupted interior prayer is the only perfect criterion of good and evil. Everything which does not interrupt it is permitted, everything which interrupts it is forbidden. It is impossible to do harm to others when we act in a state of prayer—on condition that it is true prayer. But before reaching that stage, we must have worn down our own will against the observance of rules.

Hope is the knowledge that the evil we bear within us is finite, that the slightest turning of the will towards good, though it should last but an instant, destroys a little of it, and that, in the spiritual realm, everything good infallibly produces good. Those who do not know this are doomed to the torture of the Danaïds.

Good infallibly produces good, and evil evil, in the purely spiritual realm. On the other hand, in the natural realm, that of psychology included, good and evil reciprocally produce each other. Accordingly we cannot have security until we have reached the spiritual realm—precisely the realm where we can obtain nothing by our own efforts, where we must wait for everything to come to us from outside.

INTELLIGENCE AND GRACE

We know by means of our intelligence that what the intelligence does not comprehend is more real than what it does comprehend.

Faith is experience that intelligence is enlightened by love.

Only, intelligence has to recognize by the methods proper to it, that is to say by verification and demonstration, the pre-eminence of love. It must not yield unless it knows why, and it must know this quite precisely and clearly. Otherwise its submission is a mistake and that to which it submits itself is something other than supernatural love. For example it may be social influence.

In the intellectual order, the virtue of humility is nothing more nor less than the power of attention.

The wrong humility leads us to believe that we are nothing in so far as we are ourselves—in so far as we are certain particular human beings.

True humility is the knowledge that we are nothing in so far as we are human beings as such, and, more generally, in so far as we are creatures. The intelligence plays a great part in this. We have to form a conception of the universal.

When we listen to Bach or to a Gregorian melody, all the faculties of the soul become tense and silent in order to apprehend this thing of perfect beauty—each after its own fashion—the intelligence among the rest. It finds nothing in this thing it hears to affirm or deny, but it feeds upon it.

Should not faith be an adherence of this kind?

The mysteries of faith are degraded if they are made into an object of affirmation and negation, when in reality they should be an object of contemplation.

The privileged rôle of the intelligence in real love comes from the fact that it is inherent in the nature of intelligence to become obliterated through the very fact that it is exercised. I can make efforts to discover truths, but when I have them before me they exist and I do not count.

There is nothing nearer to true humility than the intelligence. It is impossible to be proud of our intelligence at the moment when we are really exercising it. Moreover, when we do exercise it we are not attached to it, for we know that even if we became an idiot the following instant and remained so for the rest of our life, the truth would continue unchanged.

The mysteries of the Catholic faith are not intended to be believed by all the parts of the soul. The presence of Christ in the host is not a fact of the same kind as the presence of Paul's soul in Paul's body (actually both are completely incomprehensible, but not in the same way). The Eucharist should not then be an object of belief for the part of me which apprehends facts. That is where Protestantism is true. But this presence of Christ in the host is not a symbol, for a symbol is the combination of an abstraction and an image, it is something which human intelligence can represent to itself, it is not supernatural. There the Catholics are right, not the Protestants. Only with that part of us which is made for the supernatural should we adhere to these mysteries.

The rôle of the intelligence—that part of us which affirms and denies and formulates opinions—is merely to submit. All that I conceive of as true is less true than those things of which I cannot conceive the truth, but which I love. Saint John of the Cross calls faith a night. With those who have had a Christian education, the lower parts of the soul become attached to these mysteries when they have no right to do so. That is why such people need a purification of which Saint John of the Cross describes the stages. Atheism and incredulity constitute an equivalent of this purification.

The desire to discover something new prevents people from allowing their thoughts to dwell on the transcendent, undemonstrable meaning of what has already been discovered. My total lack of talent which makes such a desire out of the question for me is a great favour I have received. The recognized and accepted lack of intellectual gifts compels the disinterested use of the intelligence.

The object of our search should not be the supernatural, but the world. The supernatural is light itself: if we make an object of it we lower it.

The world is a text with several meanings, and we pass from one meaning to another by a process of work. It must be work in which the body constantly bears a part, as, for example, when we learn the alphabet of a foreign language: this alphabet has to enter into our hand by dint of forming the letters. If this condition is not fulfilled, every change in our way of thinking is illusory.

We have not to choose between opinions. We have to welcome them all but arrange them vertically, placing them on suitable levels.

Thus: chance, destiny, Providence.

Intelligence can never penetrate the mystery, but it, and it alone, can judge of the suitability of the words which express it. For this task it needs to be keener, more discerning, more precise, more exact and more exacting than for any other.

The Greeks believed that only truth was suitable for divine things—not error nor approximations. The divine character of anything made them more exacting with regard to accuracy. (We do precisely the opposite, warped as we are by the habit of propaganda.) It was because they saw geometry as a divine revelation that they invented a rigorous system of demonstration . . .

In all that has to do with the relations between man and the supernatural we have to seek for a more than mathematical precision; this should be more exact than science.[1]

We must suppose the rational in the Cartesian sense, that is to say

[1] Here again is one of those contradictions which can only be resolved in the realm of the inexpressible: the mystic life, which only arises from the divine arbitrariness, is nevertheless subject to the most severe rules. Saint John of the Cross was able to give a geometric plan of the journey of the soul towards God. [Editor's note.]

mechanical rule or necessity in its humanly demonstrable form, to be everywhere it is possible to suppose it, in order to bring to light that which lies outside its range.

The use of reason makes things transparent to the mind. We do not, however, see what is transparent. We see that which is opaque through the transparent—the opaque which was hidden when the transparent was not transparent. We see either the dust on the window or the view beyond the window, but never the window itself. Cleaning off the dust only serves to make the view visible. The reason should be employed only to bring us to the true mysteries, the true undemonstrables, which are reality. The uncomprehended hides the incomprehensible and should on this account be eliminated.

Science, today, will either have to seek a source of inspiration higher than itself or perish.

Science only offers three kinds of interest: (1) Technical applications, (2) A game of chess, (3) A road to God. (Attractions are added to the game of chess in the shape of competitions, prizes and medals.)

Pythagoras. Only the mystical conception of geometry could supply the degree of attention necessary for the beginning of such a science. Is it not recognized, moreover, that astronomy issues from astrology and chemistry from alchemy? But we interpret this filiation as an advance, whereas there is a degradation of the attention in it. Transcendental astrology and alchemy are the contemplation of eternal truths in the symbols offered by the stars and the combinations of substances. Astronomy and chemistry are degradations of them. When astrology and alchemy become forms of magic they are still lower degradations of them. Attention only reaches its true dimensions when it is religious.

Galileo. Having as its principle unlimited straight movement and no longer circular movement, modern science could no longer be a bridge towards God.

The philosophical cleansing of the Catholic religion has never been done. In order to do it it would be necessary to be inside and outside.

READINGS[1]

Others. To see each human being (an image of oneself) as a prison in which a prisoner dwells, surrounded by the whole universe.

Electra, daughter of a powerful father, yet reduced to slavery, hoping only in her brother, sees a young man who tells her of the death of this brother—and at the moment when her distress is utterly complete it is revealed that this young man himself is her brother.

'She, supposing him to be the gardener, . . .

We must recognize our brother in a stranger, and God in the universe.

Justice. To be ever ready to admit that another person is some-

---

[1] With Simone Weil this word means: emotional interpretation, the concrete judgment of value. For instance, I see a man climbing over a wall: instinctively, and perhaps wrongly; I 'read' in him a robber.   [Editor's note.]

thing quite different from what we read when he is there (or when we think about him). Or rather, to read in him that he is certainly something different, perhaps something completely different, from from what we read in him.

Every being cries out silently to be read differently.

We read, but also *we are read by*, others. Interferences in these readings. Forcing someone to read himself as we read him (slavery). Forcing others to read us as we read ourselves (conquest). A mechanical process. More often than not a dialogue between deaf people.

Charity and injustice can only be defined by readings, and thus no definition fits them. The miracle of the good thief was not that he thought of God, but that he recognized God in his neighbour. Peter, before the cock crew, no longer recognized God in Christ.

Others are slain for the sake of false prophets in whom they mistakenly read God.

Who can flatter himself that he will read aright?

We can be unjust through the will to offend justice or through a wrong reading of justice—but the second is nearly always the case.

What love of justice is a guarantee against a bad reading?

What is the difference between the just and the unjust if all invariably act according to the justice they read?

Joan of Arc: those who declaim about her today would nearly all have condemned her. Moreover, her judges did not condemn the saint, the virgin, etc., but the witch, the heretic, etc.[1]

Causes of wrong reading: public opinion, the passions.

---

[1] Cf. the texts of the Gospel concerning those who read wrongly: 'Father forgive them, for they know not what they do.' 'The hour will come when whoever killeth you will think that he doeth God service.' [Editor's note.]

Public opinion is a very strong cause. People read in the story of Joan of Arc what contemporary public opinion dictates. But it has been uncertain. And Christ . . .

In fictitious moral problems, calumny plays no part.

What hope is there for innocence if it is not recognized?

Readings. Reading—except where there is a certain quality of attention—obeys the law of gravity. We read the opinions suggested by gravity (the preponderant part played by the passions and by social conformity in the judgments we form of men and events).

With a higher quality of attention our reading discovers gravity itself, and various systems of possible balance.

Superposed readings: To read necessity behind sensation, to read order behind necessity, to read God behind order.

'Judge not': Christ himself does not judge. He is our judgment. Suffering innocence is the measure.

Judgment; perspective. In this sense all judgment judges him who forms it. Not to judge. This is not indifference or abstention, it is transcendent judgment, the imitation of that divine judgment which is not possible for us.

THE RING OF GYGES

We give the faults of other civilizations as a proof of the inadequacy of the religions on which they depend. Yet if we look at the record of Europe for the last twenty centuries we have no difficulty in finding faults which are at least equivalent to theirs. The destruction of America by massacre and of Africa by slavery, the massacres in the South of France—surely these things are no better than the homosexuality in Greece or the orgiastic rites of the Orient. But it is said that in Europe the blemishes existed in spite of the perfection of Christianity and that in the other civilizations they existed because of the imperfection of religion.

An outstanding example, to be carefully pondered, of the technique of error—setting aside. In estimating the value of India or Greece, we compare the good with the evil. In estimating the value of Christianity, we set the evil aside.[1]

---

[1] Simone Weil here illustrates a profound truth by a somewhat ill-chosen example. When a Christian (an Inquisitor for instance) behaves with cruelty it is quite permissible to say that he is acting in such a way in spite of his religion,

We set things aside without knowing we are doing so; that is precisely where the danger lies. Or, which is still worse, we set them aside by an act of the will, but by an act of the will that is furtive in relation to ourselves. Afterwards we do not any longer know that we have set anything aside. We do not want to know it, and, by dint of not wanting to know it, we reach the point of not being able to know it.

This faculty of setting things aside opens the door to every sort of crime. Outside those departments where education and training have forged solid links, it provides a key to absolute licence. That is what makes it possible for men to behave in such an incoherent fashion, particularly wherever the social, collective emotions play a part (war, national or class hatreds, patriotism for a party or a church). Whatever is surrounded with the prestige of the social element is set in a different place from other things and is exempt from certain connexions.

We also make use of this key when we give way to the allurements of pleasure.

I use it when, day after day, I put off the fulfilment of some obligation. I separate the obligation and the passage of time.

There is nothing more desirable than to get rid of this key. It should be thrown to the bottom of a well whence it can never again be recovered.

The ring of Gyges who has become invisible—this is precisely the act of setting aside: setting oneself aside from the crime one commits; not establishing the connexion between the two.

The act of throwing away the key, of throwing away the ring of Gyges—this is the effort proper to the will. It is the act by which, in pain and blindness, we make our way out of the cave.

Gyges: 'I have become king, and the other king has been

since his religion enjoins charity above all things. When, however, a Nazi acts in the same way it is allowable to attribute his conduct (at least in part) to his doctrine, since his doctrine permits it. [Editor's note.]

assassinated.' No connexion whatever between these two things. There we have the ring!

The owner of a factory: 'I enjoy this and that expensive luxury and my workmen are miserably poor.' He may be very sincerely sorry for his workmen and yet not form the connexion.

For no connexion is formed if thought does not bring it about. Two and two remain indefinitely as two and two unless thought adds them together to make them into four.

We hate the people who try to make us form the connexions we do not want to form.

Justice consists of establishing between analogous things connexions identical with those between similar terms, even when some of these things concern us personally and are an object of attachment for us.

This virtue is situated at the point of contact of the natural and the supernatural. It belongs to the realm of the will and of clear understanding, hence it is part of the cave (for our clarity is a twilight), but we cannot hold on to it unless we pass into the light.

MEANING OF THE UNIVERSE[1]

We are a part which has to imitate the whole.

The ātman. Let the soul of a man take the whole universe for its body. Let its relation to the whole universe be like that of a collector to his collection, or of one of the soldiers who died crying out 'Long live the Emperor!' to Napoleon. The soul transports itself outside the actual body into something else. Let it therefore transport itself into the whole universe.

We should identify ourselves with the universe itself. Everything that is less than the universe is subject to suffering.

Even though I die, the universe continues. That does not console me if I am anything other than the universe. If, however, the

---

[1] The identification of the soul with the universe has no connexion here with pantheism. One can only fully accept the blind necessity which rules the universe by holding closely through love to the God who transcends the universe. Cf. above: 'This world, in so far as it is quite empty of God, is God himself.' [Editor's a note.]

universe is, as it were, another body to my soul, my death ceases to have any more importance for me than that of a stranger. The same is true of my sufferings.

Let the whole universe be for me, in relation to my body, what the stick of a blind man is in relation to his hand. His sensibility is really no longer in his hand but at the end of the stick. An apprenticeship is necessary.

To limit one's love to the pure object is the same thing as to extend it to the whole universe.

To change the relationship between ourselves and the world in the same way as, through apprenticeship, the workman changes the relationship between himself and the tool. Getting hurt: this is the trade entering into the body. May all suffering make the universe enter into the body.

Habit, skill: a transference of the consciousness into an object other than the body itself.

May this object be the universe, the seasons, the sun, the stars.

The relationship between the body and the tool changes during apprenticeship. We have to change the relationship between our body and the world.

We do not become detached, we change our attachment. We must attach ourselves to the all.

We have to feel the universe through each sensation. What does it matter then whether it be pleasure or pain? If our hand is shaken by a beloved friend when we meet again after a long separation, what does it matter that he squeezes it hard and hurts us?

There is a degree of pain on reaching which we lose the world. But afterwards peace comes. And if the paroxysm returns, so does the peace which follows it. If we realize this, that very degree of pain turns into an expectation of peace, and as a result does not break our contact with the world.

Two tendencies with opposite extremes: to destroy the self for the sake of the universe, or to destroy the universe for the sake of the self. He who has not been able to become nothing runs the risk of reaching a moment when everything other than himself ceases to exist.

External necessity or an inner need as imperative as that of breathing. 'Let us become the central breath.' Even if a pain in our chest makes respiration extremely painful, we still breathe, we cannot help it.

We have to associate the rhythm of the life of the body with that of the world, to feel this association constantly and to feel also the perpetual exchange of matter by which the human being bathes in the world.

Things which nothing can take from a human being as long as he lives: in the way of movement over which his will has a hold, respiration; in the way of perception, space (even in a dungeon, even with our eyes blinded and our ear-drums pierced, as long as we live we are aware of space).

We have to attach to these things the thoughts which we desire that no circumstances should be able to deprive us of.

To love our neighbour as ourselves does not mean that we should love all people equally, for I do not have an equal love for all the modes of existence of myself. Nor does it mean that we should never make them suffer, for I do not refuse to make myself suffer. But we should have with each person the relationship of one conception of the universe to another conception of the universe, and not to a part of the universe.

Not to accept an event in the world is to wish that the world did not exist. That is within my power—for myself. If I wish it I obtain it. I am then an excrescence produced by the world.

Wishes in folklore: what makes wishes dangerous is the fact that they are granted.

To wish that the world did not exist is to wish that I, just as I am, may be everything.

Would that the entire universe, from this pebble at my feet to the most distant stars, existed for me at every moment as much as Agnès did for Arnolphe or his money-box did for Harpagon.

If I choose, the world can belong to me like the treasure does to the miser.

But it is a treasure that does not increase.

This irreducible 'I' which is the irreducible basis of my suffering—I have to make this 'I' universal.

What does it matter that there should never be joy in me since there is perfect joy perpetually in God! And the same is true with regard to beauty, intelligence and all things.

To desire one's salvation is wrong, not because it is selfish (it is not in man's power to be selfish), but because it is an orientation of the soul towards a merely particular and contingent possibility instead of towards a completeness of being, instead of towards the good which exists unconditionally.

All that I wish for exists, or has existed, or will exist somewhere. For I am incapable of complete invention. In that case how should I not be satisfied?

Br . . . I could not prevent myself from imagining him living, imagining his house as a possible place for me to listen to his delightful conversation. Thus the consciousness of the fact of his death made a frightful desert. Cold with metallic coldness. What did it matter to me that there were other people to love? The love that I directed towards him, together with the outlines shaping in my mind of exchanges of ideas which could take place with no one else, were without an object. Now I no longer imagine him as alive and his death has ceased to be intolerable for me. The memory of him is sweet to me. But there are others whom I did not know then and whose death would affect me in the same way.

D . . . is not dead, but the friendship that I bore him is dead, and a like sorrow goes with it. He is no more than a shadow.

But I cannot imagine the same transformation for X . . ., Y . . ., Z . . ., who, nevertheless, so short a time ago did not exist in my consciousness.

Just as parents find it impossible to realize that three years ago their child was non-existent, I find it impossible to realize that I have not always known the beings I love.

I think I must love wrongly: otherwise things would not seem like this to me. My love would not be attached to a few beings. It would be extended to everything which is worthy of love.

'Be ye perfect even as your Father who is in heaven. . . .' Love in the same way as the sun gives light. Love has to be brought back to ourselves in order that it may be shed on all things. God alone loves all things and he only loves himself.

To love in God is far more difficult than we think.

I can taint the whole universe with my wretchedness without feeling it or collecting it together within myself.

We have to endure the discordance between imagination and fact.

It is better to say 'I am suffering' than 'this landscape is ugly'.

We must not want to change our own weight in the balance of the world—the golden balance of Zeus.

The whole cow gives milk although the milk is only drawn from the udder. In the same way the world is the producer of saintliness.

METAXU

All created things refuse to be for me as ends. Such is God's extreme mercy towards me. And that very thing is what constitutes evil. Evil is the form which God's mercy takes in this world.

This world is the closed door. It is a barrier. And at the same time it is the way through.

Two prisoners whose cells adjoin communicate with each other by knocking on the wall. The wall is the thing which separates them but it is also their means of communication. It is the same with us and God. Every separation is a link.

By putting all our desire for good into a thing we make that thing a condition of our existence. But we do not on that account make of it a good. Merely to exist is not enough for us.

The essence of created things is to be intermediaries. They are intermediaries leading from one to the other and there is no end to this. They are intermediaries leading to God. We have to experience them as such.

The bridges of the Greeks. We have inherited them but we do not know how to use them. We thought they were intended to have houses built upon them. We have erected skyscrapers on them to which we ceaselessly add storeys. We no longer know that they are bridges, things made so that we may pass along them, and that by passing along them we go towards God.

Only he who loves God with a supernatural love can look upon means simply as means.

Power (and money, power's master key) is means at its purest. For that very reason, it is the supreme end for all those who have not understood.

This world, the realm of necessity, offers us absolutely nothing except means. Our will is for ever sent from one means to another like a billiard ball.

All our desires are contradictory, like the desire for food. I want the person I love to love me. If, however, he is totally devoted to me, he does not exist any longer, and I cease to love him. And as long as he is not totally devoted to me he does not love me enough. Hunger and repletion.

Desire is evil and illusory, yet without desire we should not seek for that which is truly absolute, truly boundless. We have to have experienced it. Misery of those beings from whom fatigue takes away that supplementary energy which is the source of desire.

Misery also of those who are blinded by desire.

We have to fix our desire to the axis of the poles.

What is it a sacrilege to destroy? Not that which is base, for that is of no importance. Not that which is high, for, even should we want to, we cannot touch that. The *metaxu*. The *metaxu* form the region of good and evil.

No human being should be deprived of his *metaxu*, that is to say of those relative and mixed blessings (home, country, traditions, culture, etc.) which warm and nourish the soul and without which, short of sainthood, a *human* life is not possible.

The true earthly blessings are *metaxu*. We can respect those of others only in so far as we regard those we ourselves possess as *metaxu*. This implies that we are already making our way towards the point where it is possible to do without them. For example, if we are to respect foreign countries, we must make of our own country, not an idol, but a stepping-stone towards God.

All the faculties being freely exercised without becoming mixed, starting from a single, unique principle. It is the microcosm, the imitation of the world. Christ according to Saint Thomas. The just man of the Republic. When Plato speaks of specialization he speaks of the specialization of man's faculties and not of the specialization of men; the same applies to hierarchy. The temporal having no meaning except by and for the spiritual, but not being mixed with the spiritual—leading to it by nostalgia, by reaching beyond itself. It is the temporal seen as a bridge, a *metaxu*. It is the Greek and Provençal vocation.

Civilization of the Greeks. No adoration of force. The temporal was only a bridge. Among the states of the soul they did not seek intensity but purity.

BEAUTY

Beauty is the harmony of chance and the good.

Beauty is necessity which, while remaining in conformity with its own law and with that alone, is obedient to the good.

The subject of science is the beautiful (that is to say order, proportion, harmony) in so far as it is suprasensible and necessary.
    The subject of art is sensible and contingent beauty discerned through the network of chance and evil.

The beautiful in nature is a union of the sensible impression and of the sense of necessity. Things must be like that (in the first place), and, precisely, they are like that.

Beauty captivates the flesh in order to obtain permission to pass right to the soul.

Among other unions of contraries found in beauty there is that of the instantaneous and the eternal.

The beautiful is that which we can contemplate. A statue, a picture which we can gaze at for hours.

The beautiful is something on which we can fix our attention. Gregorian music. When the same things are sung for hours each day and every day, whatever falls even slightly short of supreme excellence becomes unendurable and is eliminated.

The Greeks looked at their temples. We can endure the statues in the Luxembourg because we do not look at them.

A picture such as one could place in the cell of a criminal sentenced to solitary confinement for life without it being an atrocity, on the contrary.

Only drama without movement is truly beautiful. Shakespeare's tragedies are second-class with the exception of *Lear*. Those of Racine, third-class except for *Phèdre*. Those of Corneille of the nth class.

A work of art has an author and yet, when it is perfect, it has something which is essentially anonymous about it. It imitates the anonymity of divine art. In the same way the beauty of the world proves there to be a God who is personal and impersonal at the same time and is neither the one nor the other separately.

The beautiful is a carnal attraction which keeps us at a distance and implies a renunciation. This includes the renunciation of that which is most deep-seated, the imagination. We want to eat all the other objects of desire. The beautiful is that which we desire without wishing to eat it. We desire that it should be.

We have to remain quite still and unite ourselves with that which we desire yet do not approach.

We unite ourselves to God in this way: we cannot approach him.

Distance is the soul of the beautiful.

The attitude of looking and waiting is the attitude which corresponds with the beautiful. As long as one can go on conceiving, wishing, longing, the beautiful does not appear. That is why in all beauty we find contradiction, bitterness and absence which are irreducible.

Poetry: *impossible* pain and joy. A poignant touch, nostalgia. Such is Provençal and English poetry. A joy which by reason of its unmixed purity hurts, a pain which by reason of its unmixed purity brings peace.

Beauty: a fruit which we look at without trying to seize it.
    The same with an affliction which we contemplate without drawing back.

A double movement of descent: to do again, out of love, what gravity does. Is not the double movement of descent the key to all art?[1]

This movement of descent, the mirror of grace, is the essence of all music. All the rest only serves to enshrine it.
    The rising of the notes is a purely sensorial rising. The descent is at the same time a sensorial descent and a spiritual rising. Here we have the paradise which every being longs for: where the slope of nature makes us rise towards the good.

In everything which gives us the pure authentic feeling of beauty there really is the presence of God. There is as it were an incarnation of God in the world and it is indicated by beauty.
    The beautiful is the experimental proof that the incarnation is possible.
    Hence all art of the highest order is religious in essence. (That

---

[1] *Descendit ad inferos* . . . So, in another order, great art redeems gravity by espousing it out of love.   [Editor's note.]

is what people have forgotten today.) A Gregorian melody is as powerful a witness as the death of a martyr.

If the beautiful is the real presence of God in matter and if contact with the beautiful is a sacrament in the full sense of the word, how is it that there are so many perverted aesthetes? Nero. Is it like the hunger of those who frequent black masses for the consecrated hosts? Or is it, more probably, because these people do not devote themselves to what is genuinely beautiful, but to a bad imitation? For, just as there, is an art which is divine, so there is one which is demoniacal. It was no doubt the latter that Nero loved. A great deal of our art is of the devil.

A person who is passionately fond of music may quite well be a perverted person—but I should find it hard to believe this of any one who thirsted for Gregorian chanting.

We must certainly have committed crimes which have made us accursed, since we have lost all the poetry of the universe.

Art has no immediate future because all art is collective and there is no more collective life (there are only dead collections of people), and also because of this breaking of the true pact between the body and the soul. Greek art coincided with the beginning of geometry and with athleticism, the art of the Middle Ages with the craftsmen's guilds, the art of the Renaissance with the beginning of mechanics, etc. . . . Since 1914 there has been a complete cut. Even comedy is almost impossible. There is only room for satire (when was it easier to understand Juvenal?). Art will never be reborn except from amidst a general anarchy— it will be epic no doubt, because affliction will have simplified a great many things. . . . Is it therefore quite useless for you to envy Leonardo or Bach. Greatness in our times must take a different course. Moreover it can only be solitary, obscure and without an echo . . . (but without an echo, no art).

ALGEBRA

Money, mechanization, algebra. The three monsters of contemporary civilization. Complete analogy.

Algebra and money are essentially levellers, the first intellectually, the second effectively.

About fifty years ago the life of the Provençal peasants ceased to be like that of the Greek peasants described by Hesiod. The destruction of science as conceived by the Greeks took place at about the same period. Money and algebra triumphed simultaneously.

The relation of the sign to the thing signified is being destroyed, the game of exchanges between signs is being multiplied of itself and for itself. And the increasing complication demands that there should be signs for signs. . . .

Among the characteristics of the modern world we must not

forget the impossibility of thinking in concrete terms of the relationship between effort and the result of effort. There are too many intermediaries. As in the other cases, this relationship which does not lie in any thought, lies in a thing: money.

As collective thought cannot exist as thought, it passes into things (signs, machines . . .). Hence the paradox: it is the thing which thinks and the man who is reduced to the state of a thing.

There is no collective thought. On the other hand our science is collective like our technics. Specialization. We inherit not only results but methods which we do not understand. For the matter of that the two are inseparable, for the results of algebra provide methods for the other sciences.

To make an inventory or criticism of our civilization—what does that mean? To try to expose in precise terms the trap which has made man the slave of his own inventions. How has unconsciousness infiltrated itself into methodical thought and action? To escape by a return to the primitive state is a lazy solution. We have to rediscover the original pact between the spirit and the world in this very civilization of which we form a part. But it is a task which is beyond our power on account of the shortness of life and the impossibility of collaboration and of succession. That is no reason for not undertaking it. The situation of all of us is comparable to that of Socrates when he was awaiting death in his prison and began to learn to play the lyre. . . . At any rate we shall have lived. . . .

The spirit, overcome by the weight of quantity, has no longer any other criterion than efficiency.

Modern life is given over to immoderation. Immoderation invades everything: actions and thought, public and private life.

The decadence of art is due to it. There is no more balance anywhere. The Catholic movement is to some extent in reaction against this; the Catholic ceremonies, at least, have remained intact. But then they are unrelated to the rest of existence.

Capitalism has brought about the emancipation of collective humanity with respect to nature. But this collective humanity has itself taken on with respect to the individual the oppressive function formerly exercised by nature.

This is true even with material things: fire, water etc. The community has taken possession of all these natural forces.

Question: can this emancipation, won by society, be transferred to the individual?

THE SOCIAL IMPRINT[1]

Man is a slave in so far as between action and its effect, between effort and the finished work, there is the interference of alien wills.

This is the case both with the slave *and* the master today. Never can man deal directly with the conditions of his own action. Society forms a screen between nature and man.

To be in direct contact with nature and not with men is the only discipline. To be dependent on an alien will is to be a slave. This, however, is the fate of all men. The slave is dependent on the master and the master on the slave. This is a situation which makes us either servile or tyrannical or both at once (*omnia serviliter pro dominatione*). On the contrary, when we are face to face with inert nature our only resource is to think.

---

[1] The title of this chapter is *La Lettre Sociale*—cf. Alfred de Vigny:
Si tu frémis de voir sur ton épaule
La lettre sociale écrite avec du fer . . .

The notion of oppression is, in short, a stupidity: one only has to read the *Iliad*. And the notion of an oppressive class is even more stupid. We can only speak of an oppressive structure of society.

The difference between a slave and a citizen (Montesquieu, Rousseau . . .): a slave is subject to his master and a citizen to the laws. It may happen that the master is very gentle and the laws very harsh: that changes nothing. Everything lies in the distance between caprice and rule.

Why is subordination to caprice slavery? The root cause is found in the relation between the soul and time. He who is subject to the arbitrary is suspended on the thread of time; he has to wait (the most humiliating situation possible . . .) for what the following moment will bring him. He does not dispose of his moments; for him the present is no longer a lever by which he can bring pressure to bear on the future.

To have to deal directly with things frees the spirit. To have to deal directly with men debases us if we are dependent on them, whether this dependence be in the form of submission or of command.

Why these men between Nature and me?

Never to have to take into account an unknown thought . . . (for then we are given over to chance).

Remedy: apart from the ties of brotherhood, to treat men like a spectacle and *never* seek for friendship; to live in the midst of men as in that crowded railway carriage between Saint-Etienne and Le Puy. . . . Above all never to allow oneself to dream of friendship. Everything has to be paid for. Rely only on yourself.

The powerful, if they carry oppression beyond a certain point, necessarily end by making themselves *adored* by their slaves. For the thought of being under absolute compulsion, the plaything of another, is unendurable for a human being. Hence, if every way of escape from this constraint is taken from him, there is nothing left for him to do but to persuade himself that he does the things he is forced to do willingly, that is to say, to substitute *devotion* for *obedience*. And sometimes he will even strive to do more than he is obliged and will suffer less thereby, in the same way as children when they are playing will endure with a laugh physical suffering which they would find unbearable if it were inflicted on them as a punishment. It is by this twist that slavery debases the soul: this devotion is in fact based on a lie, since the reasons for it cannot bear investigation. (In this respect the Catholic principle of obedience should be considered as a liberating principle, whereas Protestantism is based on the idea of sacrifice and devotion.) The only way of salvation is to replace the unendurable idea of compulsion, not by the illusion of devotion, but by the notion of necessity.

On the other hand revolt, if it does not immediately pass into definite and effective action, is always changed into its opposite through the feeling of utter impotence which results from it. In other words the chief support of the oppressor lies precisely in the unavailing revolt of the oppressed.

It would be possible to write the novel of a conscript of Napoleon from this point of view.

Moreover, the master is deceived too by the fallacy of devotion.

We must always consider men in power as dangerous things. We must keep out of their way as much as we can without losing our self-respect. And if one day we are driven, under pain of cowardice, to go and break ourselves against their power, we must consider ourselves as vanquished by the nature of things and not by men. One can be in a prison cell and in chains, but one can also be smitten with blindness or paralysis. There is no difference.

The only way to preserve our dignity when submission is

forced upon us is to consider our chief as a thing. Every man is the slave of necessity, but the conscious slave is far superior.

Social problem. To limit to the minimum the proportion of the supernatural indispensable to make the atmosphere of social life possible to breathe. Everything which tends to increase it is bad (it is tempting God).

We must eliminate affliction as much as we can from social life, for affliction only serves the purposes of grace and society is not a society of the elect. There will always be enough affliction for the elect.

ISRAEL

Christendom has become totalitarian, conquering, and exterminating, because it has not developed the idea of God's absence and non-activity here below. It has attached itself to Jehovah no less than to Christ, and conceived of Providence in the manner of the Old Testament. Only Israel could stand up to Rome, because it resembled it; and this is how the birth of Christianity was marked with the Roman stain before it became the official religion of the Empire. The evil done by Rome has never been truly redressed.

God's promises to Moses and Joshua were purely temporal, made at a time when Egypt was moving towards the eternal salvation of the soul. Having refused the Egyptian revelation, the Hebrews got the God they deserved: a carnal and collective God who, right up to the exile, did not speak (except in the Psalms?) to a single soul. . . . The only pure individuals in the poems of the Old Testament are Abel, Enoch, Noah, Melchisedek, Job, and Daniel. It is not surprising that little could be expected of such a people, fugitive slaves, conquerors of a paradise which had been fashioned by civilizations in whose labour they had not shared and which they destroyed through massacres. To speak of an 'educational God' in connection with this people is a cruel joke.

It is not astonishing that there should be so much evil in a civilization—ours—contaminated to the core, in its very inspiration, by this terrible lie. The curse of Israel rests on Christendom. Israel meant atrocities, the Inquisition, the extermination of heretics and infidels. Israel meant (and to a certain extent still does . . .) capitalism. Israel means totalitarianism, especially with regard to its worst enemies.

There can be no personal contact between man and God except through the person of the Mediator. Without the latter, God can only be present to man collectively, nationally. Israel chose the national God and simultaneously rejected the Mediator; it may, at one time or another, have moved towards true monotheism, but it always fell back on, and was unable not to fall back on, the God of the tribe.

Anyone who has contact with the supernatural is essentially sovereign, for in the form of the infinitely small he is a presence in society which transcends the social order.

But the place he occupies in the social hierarchy is completely immaterial. As for what is great in the social order, only he is capable of it who who has harnessed a large part of the Great Beast's energy. But he can have no share in the supernatural.

Moses, Joshuah—that is the share in the supernatural of those who have harnessed much social energy. Israel was an attempt at supernatural social life. No country, presumably, has suceeded better at this kind of thing. Useless to start again. The result shows just what sort of divine revelation the Great Beast is capable of.

Isaiah the first to bring pure illumination.

Israel stood up to Rome because its God, even though immaterial, was a temporal sovereign on a par with the Emperor, and
thanks to this Christianity could be born. The religion of Israel
was not noble enough to be fragile, and due to its solidity could
protect belief in the most elevated.[1]

For the Passion to be possible, it was necessary that Israel ignore
the idea of the Incarnation. Rome, too (these were, perhaps, the
only two peoples to ignore it). But it was necessary that Israel
have some share in God. As great a share as possible without
being spiritual or supernatural. Exclusively collective religion. It
was because of this ignorance, this darkness, that it became the
chosen people. So one can understand Isaiah, 'I have hardenend
their hearts, so that they may not hear my words.'

That is why, in Israel, everything is sullied by sin, as there is
no purity without participating in the divine incarnation, so that
a lack of such participation should be obvious.

Jacob's struggle with the angel – is not this the great blemish?
'The Eternal . . . will do justice to Jacob according to his works.
In his mother's womb did he already displace his brother, and,
in his manliness, triumph over a God. He fought against an angel
and was vanquished, and here he cries and asks for mercy . . .'
Isn't this the great tragedy, to battle against God and not to be
vanquished?

Israel. From Abraham onwards (including himself, but excepting
some of the prophets), and as though it had been planned,
everything becomes sullied and foul, as if to demonstrate quite
clearly: Look! There it is, evil!

[1] Note, as Simone Weil does here, that on the one hand the history of Israel
contains flashes of pure mysticism (Isaiah, etc.); and that, on the other hand,
incipient Christanity was protected by its Jewish 'shell'. This is already to
legitimate Israel's divine mission.

A people chosen for its blindness, chosen to be Christ's executioner.

The Jews, that handful of uprooted people, have caused the uprootedness of the whole terrestrial globe. Their involvement in Christianity has made of Christendom, in regard to its own past, something uprooted. The orientation of the Enlightenment, 1789, secularism, etc. have infinitely increased this uprooting, through the lie of progress. And uprooted Europe has uprooted the rest of the world, by colonial conquest. Capitalism, totalitarianism, have a share in this progressive uprootedness; the antisemites, naturally, propagate the Jewish influence. But before Assyria in the Orient and Rome in the Occident uprooted through poison, they had already uprooted with the broadsword.

It was primitive Christianity that fabricated the poisonous idea of progress, through the notion of a divine education that was to mould man and enable him to receive the message of Christ. This accorded with the expectation as imminent phenomena of a universal conversion of nations and the end of the world. But as neither of these had come about, the notion of progress was, after seventeen centuries, extended beyond the moment of the Christian Revelation. At this point, it had to turn itself against Christianity.

The other poisons mixed with the truth in Christianity are Jewish in origin. The former is specifically Christian.

The metaphor of a divine education dissolves the individual destiny, which alone matters for salvation, into the destiny of a people.

Christianity wanted to look for a harmony in history. This is the germ of Hegel and Marx. The notion of history as a directed continuity is a Christian notion.

It seems to me that few ideas could be more utterly mistaken.

Looking for harmony in the future, in what is contrary to eternity. Bad union of contraries.

Humanism and what has arisen out of it, is not a return to antiquity, but a development of poisons that are internal to Christianity.

It is supernatural love that is free. In trying to force it, one substitutes for it a natural love. Conversely, however, freedom without supernatural love—that of 1789—is entirely empty, a simple abstraction, with no possibility of ever becoming real.

THE GREAT BEAST

The Great Beast[1] is the only object of idolatry, the only *ersatz* of God, the only imitation of something which is infinitely far from me and which is I myself.

If we could be egoistical it would be very pleasant. It would be a rest. But literally we cannot.

It is impossible for me to take myself as an end or, in consequence, my fellow man as an end, since he is my fellow. Nor can I take any material thing, because matter is still less capable of having finality conferred upon it than human beings are.

Only one thing can be taken as an end, for in relation to the human person it possesses a kind of transcendence: this is the collective. The collective is the object of all idolatry, this it is

[1] On the origin of this myth cf. Plato, *Republic*, Book VI. To adore the 'Great Beast' is to think and act in conformity with the prejudices and reactions of the multitude to the detriment of all personal search for truth and goodness. [Editor's note.]

which chains us to the earth. In the case of avarice: gold is of the social order. In the case of ambition: power is of the social order. Science and art ate full of the social element also. And love? Love is more or less of an exception: that is why we can go to God through love, not through avarice or ambition. Yet the social element is not absent from love (passions excited by princes, celebrated people, all those who have prestige . . .).

There are two goods of the same denomination but radically different from each other: one which is the opposite of evil and one which is the absolute. The absolute has no opposite. The relative is not the opposite of the absolute; it is derived from it through a relationship which is not commutative. That which we want is the absolute good. That which is within our reach is the good which is correlated to evil. We betake ourselves to it by mistake, like the prince who starts to make love to the maid instead of the mistress. The error is due to the clothes. It is the social which throws the colour of the absolute over the relative. The remedy is in the idea of relationship. Relationship breaks its way out of the social. It is the monopoly of the individual. Society is the cave. The way out is solitude.

To relate belongs to the solitary spirit. No crowd can conceive relationship. 'This is good or bad in relation to . . .', 'in so far as . . .' That escapes the crowd. A crowd cannot add things together.

He who is above social life returns to it when he wishes, not so he who is below. It is the same with everything. A relationship which is not commutative between what is better and what is less good.

The vegetative and the social are the two realms where the good does not enter.

Christ redeemed the vegetative, not the social. He did not pray for the world.

The social order is irreducibly that of the prince of this world. Our only duty with regard to the social is to try to limit the evil of it. (Richelieu: the salvation of states lies only in this world.)

A society like the Church, which claims to be divine is perhaps more dangerous on account of the *ersatz* good which it contains than on account of the evil which sullies it.

Something of the social labelled divine: an intoxicating mixture which carries with it every sort of licence. Devil disguised.

Conscience is deceived by the social. Our supplementary energy (imaginative) is to a great extent taken up with the social. It has to be detached from it. That is the most difficult of detachments.

Meditation on the social mechanism is in this respect a purification of the first importance.

To contemplate the social is as good a way of detachment as to retire from the world. That is why I have not been wrong to rub shoulders with politics for so long.

It is only by entering the transcendental, the supernatural, the authentically spiritual order that man rises above the social. Until then, whatever he may do, the social is transcendent in relation to him.

On the non-supernatural plane, society is that which keeps evil (certain forms of it) away by forming as it were a barrier. A society of criminals or people given over to vice, even if only composed of a handful of men, destroys this barrier.

But what is it which impels people to enter such a society? Either necessity, or laxity, or, usually, a mixture of the two. They do not think they are becoming involved, for they do not know that, apart from the supernatural, it is only society which prevents us from falling naturally into the most fearful vice and crime. They do not know that they are going to become different, for they do not know the extent of the region within themselves which can be changed by environment. They always become involved without knowing.

Rome is the Great Beast of atheism and materialism, adoring nothing but itself. Israel is the Great Beast of religion. Neither the one nor the other is likable. The Great Beast is always repulsive.

Would a society in which only gravity reigned be able to exist, or is a little of the supernatural element a vital necessity?
    In Rome, perhaps, there was only gravity.
    With the Hebrews too, perhaps. Their God was heavy.

Perhaps there was only one ancient people absolutely without mysticism: Rome. By what mystery? It was an artificial city, made up of fugitives, just as Israel was.

The Great Beast of Plato. The whole of Marxism, in so far as it is true, is contained in the page of Plato on the Great Beast; and its refutation is there too.

The power of the social element. Agreement between several men brings with it a feeling of reality. It brings with it also a sense of duty. Divergence, where this agreement is concerned, appears as a sin. Hence *all* returns to the fold are possible. The state of conformity is an imitation of grace.

By a strange mystery—which is connected with the power of the social element—a profession can confer on quite ordinary men in their exercise of it, virtues which, if they were extended to all circumstances of life, would make of them heroes or saints.
    But the power of the social element makes these virtues *natural.* Accordingly they need a compensation.

Pharisees: 'Verily I say unto you, they have received their

reward.' Inversely, Christ could have said of the publicans and prostitutes: 'Verily I say unto you, they have received their punishment'—that is to say social reprobation. In so far as they have received this, the Father who is in secret does not punish them. Whereas the sins which are not accompanied by social reprobation receive their full measure of punishment from the Father who is in secret. Thus social reprobation is a favour on the part of destiny. It turns into a supplementary evil, however, for those who, under the pressure of this reprobation, manufacture for themselves eccentric social surroundings within which they have full licence. Criminal and homosexual circles, etc.

The service of the false God (of the social Beast under whatever form it may be) purifies evil by eliminating its horror. Nothing seems evil to those who serve it except failure in its service. The service of the true God, on the other hand, allows the horror of evil to remain and even makes it more intense. Whilst this evil horrifies us, we yet love it as emanating from the will of God.

Those who think today that one of the adversaries is on the side of the good, think also that that side will be victorious.[1]

To watch a good, loved as such, condemned as it were by the oncoming tide of events is an intolerable suffering.

The idea that that which does not exist any more may be a good is painful and we thrust it aside. That is submission to the Great Beast.

The force of soul of the Communists comes from the fact that they are going, not only towards what they believe to be the good, but towards what they believe will surely and soon be brought about. Thus without being saints—they are a long way from that—they can endure dangers and sufferings which only a saint would bear for justice alone.

[1] These lines were written in 1942.   [Editor's note.]

In some respects the state of mind of the Communists is very analogous to that of the early Christians.

That eschatological propaganda explains very well the persecutions of the first period.

'He to whom little is forgiven, the same loveth little.' This concerns someone with whom social virtue occupies a very large place. Grace finds little room to spare in him. Obedience to the Great Beast which conforms to the good—that is social virtue.

A Pharisee is someone who is virtuous out of obedience to the Great Beast.

Charity can and should love in every country all that is a condition of the spiritual development of individuals, that is to say, on the one hand, social order, even if it is bad, as being less bad than disorder, on the other hand the language, ceremonies, customs—all that contains beauty—all the poetry which the life of a country embraces.

But a nation as such cannot be the object of supernatural love. It has no soul. It is a Great Beast.

And yet a city . . .

But that is not social; it is a human environment of which one is no more conscious than of the air one breathes. A contact with nature, the past, tradition.

Rootedness lies in something other than the social.

Patriotism. We must not have any love other than charity. A nation cannot be an object of charity. But a country can be one—as an environment bearing traditions which are eternal. Every country can be that.

SOCIAL HARMONY

It is impossible for an order which is higher and therefore infinitely above another to be represented in it except by something infinitely small. A grain of mustard seed, an instant mirroring eternity, etc . . .

The point of contact between a circle and a straight line (a tangent). This is the presence of the higher order in the lower under the form of what is infinitely minute.

Christ is the point of tangency between humanity and God.

Unobtrusiveness—the infinitesimal character of pure good . . .

Equilibrium is the submission of one order to another, the order which transcends the first being present in it under the form of something infinitely small.

Thus a true royalty would constitute the perfect city.

Each one, in society, is the infinitely small representative of the order transcending and infinitely greater than the social.

The love of the citizen for his city and of the vassal for his lord should be a supernatural love.

Equilibrium alone destroys and annuls force. Social order can be nothing but an equilibrium of forces. As it cannot be expected that a man without grace should be just, there must be a society organized in such a way that injustices punish each other through a perpetual oscillation.

Equilibrium alone reduces force to nothing. If we know in what way society is unbalanced, we must do what we can to add weight to the lighter scale. Although the weight may consist of evil, in handling it with this intention, perhaps we do not become defiled. But we must have formed a conception of equilibrium and be ever ready to change sides like justice, 'that fugitive from the camp of conquerors'.

The meaning of the famous passage in the *Georgics* about geometry. No unlimited development is possible in the nature of things; the world is entirely based on measure and equilibrium, and it is the same with the city. All ambition is an absence of measure, absurdity.

γεωμετρίας γὰρ ἀμελεῖς.

What the ambitious man entirely forgets is the notion of relationship.

'Peuple stupide à qui ma puissance m'enchaine,
Hélas! mon orgueil même a besoin de tes bras.'[1]

The feudal bond, in making obedience a matter between one

---

[1] 'Foolish people, to whom my power enthrals me,
Alas! my very pride has need of your arms.'

man and another, greatly reduces the part played by the Great
Beast.

The law does so better still.

There should be no obedience except to the law or to a man.
That is almost what happens in the monastic orders. The city
should be built on this model.

Obedience to the overlord, to a man, but a man stripped bare,
adorned only with the majesty of the oath and not with a
majesty borrowed from the Great Beast.

A well ordered society would be one where the State only had a
negative action, comparable to that of a rudder: a light pressure
at the right moment to counteract the first suggestion of any loss
of equilibrium.

The meaning of Plato's *Politics* is that power should be in the
hands of a social group composed of conquerors and conquered.
But that is against nature except when the conquerors are bar-
barian. From this point of view the victory of barbarians over
civilized peoples, when it is not destructive, is more fruitful
than that of civilized peoples over barbarians.

Technical development, which puts force and civilization on
the same side, makes such regenerations impossible. It is accursed.

Apart from such moments of fusion, the division of power
between the strong and the weak is only possible through the
intervention of a supernatural factor.

The supernatural element in society is legitimacy in its double
form: law and the assignment of supreme power. A monarchy
tempered by laws could perhaps achieve the combination advo-
cated in the *Politics*. But there can be no legitimacy without
religion.

Obedience to a man whose authority is not illuminated by
legitimacy—that is a nightmare.

The only thing which is able to turn pure legitimacy—an idea absolutely devoid of force—into something sovereign is the thought: 'Thus it has always been and thus it will always continue to be.'

That is why a reform should always appear, either as the return to a past which has been allowed to degenerate, or as the adaptation of an institution to new conditions, an adaptation which has as its object not a change but, on the contrary, the maintenance of an unchanging relationship. For instance, supposing there were the relationship 12/4 and 4 became 5, the real conservative would not be he who wanted 12/5, but he who made 12 into 15.

The existence of a legitimate authority puts a finality into the work and actions of social life, a finality other than the thirst for one's own advancement (the only motive recognized by liberalism).

Legitimacy represents continuity in time, permanence, something unchanging. It gives as a finality to social life something which exists and which is conceived of as having always existed and as having to exist for all time. It obliges men to wish for exactly that which is.

Uprooting, the break in legitimacy, when it is not due to conquest, when it is brought about in any country as a result of the abuse of lawful authority, invariably leads men to become obsessed with the idea of progress, because finality is then turned towards the future.

Atheistic materialism is necessarily revolutionary, for, if it is to be directed towards an absolute good here on earth, it has to place it in the future. In order that this impetus should have full effect there must therefore be a mediator between the perfection to come and the present. This mediator is the chief—Lenin, etc.

He is infallible and perfectly pure. In passing through him evil becomes good.

We have either to see things in that way or to love God, or else to allow ourselves to be tossed to and fro by the little things—good and evil—of everyday life.

The link between progress and the lower level (because the aims of any generation from the moment that the preceding one has come to a stop are necessarily exterior) is an example of the kinship between force and that which is low.

The great mistake of the Marxists and of the whole of the nineteenth century was to think that by walking straight on one mounted upwards into the air.

The supreme atheistic idea is the idea of progress, which is the negation of experimental ontological proof, for it implies that the mediocre can of itself produce the best. But all modern science combines in rejecting the idea of progress. Darwin destroyed the illusion of internal progress which was found in Lamarck. The theory of mutations only leaves chance and elimination as valid. The theory of energetics postulates that energy deteriorates and never increases, and this is applicable even to vegetable and animal life.

Psychology and sociology will only become scientific through an analogous application of the notion of energy—an application incompatible with any idea of progress; then they will be resplendent with the light of true faith.

The eternal alone is invulnerable to time. In order that a work of art should be admired for all time, that a love, a friendship should last throughout a life (even stay pure for an entire day, perhaps), in order that a conception of the human condition should remain constant despite the manifold experiences and vicissitudes of fortune—there must be an inspiration from on high.

A future which is completely impossible, like the ideal of the Spanish anarchists, degrades us far less and differs far less from the eternal than a possible future. It does not even degrade us at all, except through the illusion of its possibility. If it is conceived of as impossible, it transports us into the eternal.

The possible is the realm of the imagination, and thus of degradation. We must wish either for that which actually exists or for that which cannot in any way exist—or, still better, for both. That which is and that which cannot be are both outside the realm of becoming. The past, not when the imagination takes pleasure over it but at the moment when some meeting calls it up before us in its purity, is time coloured with eternity. The feeling of reality in it is pure. There we have pure joy. There we have beauty. Proust.

We are attached to the present. We manufacture the future in our imagination. Only the past, when we do not remanufacture it, is pure reality.

Time as it flows wears down and destroys that which is temporal. Accordingly there is more of eternity in the past than in the present. The value of history properly understood is analogous to that of remembrance in Proust. Thus the past presents us with something which is at the same time real and better than ourselves, something which can draw us upwards—a thing the future never does.

The past: something real, but absolutely beyond our reach, towards which we cannot take one step, towards which we can but turn ourselves so that an emanation from it may come to us. Thus it is the most perfect image of eternal, supernatural reality.

Is it for this reason that there are joy and beauty in remembrance as such?

Whence will renewal come to us—to us who have defiled and emptied the whole earthly globe?

From the past alone, if we love it.

Contraries. Today we thirst for and are nauseated by totalitarianism, and nearly everyone loves one totalitarianism and hates another.

Is there always identity between what we love and what we hate? Do we always feel the need to love under another form that which we hate, and vice versa?

The constant illusion of Revolution consists in believing that the victims of force, being innocent of the outrages that are committed, will use force justly if it is put into their hands. But except for souls which are fairly near to saintliness, the victims are defiled by force just as their tormentors are. The evil which is in the handle of the sword is transmitted to its point. So the victims thus put in power and intoxicated by the change do as much harm or more, and soon sink back again to where they were before.

Socialism consists in imputing good to the conquered, and racialism in imputing good to the conquerors. But the revolutionary wing of socialism makes use of those who, though lowly born, are by nature and by vocation conquerors. Thus it ends up by having the same form of ethics.

Modern totalitarianism is to the Catholic totalitarianism of the twelfth century what the spirit of laïcism and freemasonry is to the humanism of the Renaissance. Humanity deteriorates at each swing of the pendulum. How far will this go?

After the collapse of our civilization there must be one of two things: either the whole of it will perish like the ancient civilizations, or it will adapt itself to a decentralized world. It rests with us, not to break up the centralization (for it automatically goes on increasing like a snowball until the catastrophe comes), but to prepare for the future.

Our period has destroyed the interior hierarchy. How should it allow the social hierarchy, which is only a clumsy image of it, to go on existing?

You could not be born at a better period than the present, when we have lost everything.

THE MYSTICISM OF WORK

The secret of the human condition is that there is no equilibrium between man and the surrounding forces of nature, which infinitely exceed him when in inaction; there is only equilibrium in action by which man recreates his own life through work.

Man's greatness is always to recreate his life, to recreate what is given to him, to fashion that very thing which he undergoes. Through work he produces his own natural existence. Through science he recreates the universe by means of symbols. Through art he recreates the alliance between his body and his soul (cf. the speech of Eupalinos). It is to be noticed that each of these three things is something poor, empty and vain taken by itself and not in relation to the two others. Union of the three: a working people's culture (that will not be just yet) . . .

Plato himself is only a forerunner. The Greeks knew about art and sport, but not about work. The master is the slave of the slave in the sense that the slave *makes* the master.

Two tasks:

To individualize machinery.

To individualize science (popularization, a people's university on the Socratic model for the study of the elements of the various trades).

Manual work. Why has there never been a mystic, workman or peasant, to write on the use to be made of disgust for work. Our souls fly from this disgust which is so often there, ever threatening, and try to hide it from themselves by reacting vegetatively. There is mortal danger in admitting it to ourselves. This is the source of the falsehood peculiar to the working classes. (There is a falsehood peculiar to each level.)

This disgust is the burdensomeness of time. To acknowledge it to ourselves without giving way under it makes us mount upwards.

Disgust in all its forms is one of the most precious trials sent to man as a ladder by which to rise. I have a very large share of this favour.

We have to turn all our disgust into a disgust for ourselves.

Monotony is the most beautiful or the most atrocious thing. The most beautiful if it is a reflection of eternity—the most atrocious if it is the sign of an unvarying perpetuity. It is time surpassed or time sterilized.

The circle is the symbol of monotony which is beautiful, the swinging of a pendulum of monotony which is atrocious.

The spirituality of work. Work makes us experience in the most exhausting manner the phenomenon of finality rebounding like a ball; to work in order to eat, to eat in order to work.

If we regard one of the two as an end, or the one and the other taken separately, we are lost. Only the cycle contains the truth.

A squirrel turning in its cage and the rotation of the celestial sphere—extreme misery and extreme grandeur.

It is when man sees himself as a squirrel turning round and round in a circular cage that, if he does not lie to himself, he is close to salvation.

The great hardship in manual work is that we are compelled to expend our efforts for such long hours simply in order to exist.

The slave is he to whom no good is proposed as the object of his labour except mere existence.

Accordingly he must either be detached or fall to the vegetative level.

No terrestrial finality separates the workers from God. They alone are so situated. All other conditions imply special aims which form a screen between man and pure good. But for them no such screen exists. They have nothing superfluous of which they have to strip themselves.

To strive from necessity and not for some good—driven not drawn—in order to maintain our existence just as it is—that is always slavery.

In this sense the slavery of manual workers is irreducible.

Effort without finality.

It is terrible—or the most beautiful thing of all—if it is finality without an end. The beautiful alone enables us to be satisfied by that which is.

Workers need poetry more than bread. They need that their life should be a poem. They need some light from eternity.

Religion alone can be the source of such poetry.

It is not religion but revolution which is the opium of the people.

Deprivation of this poetry explains all forms of demoralization.

Slavery is work without any light from eternity, without poetry, without religion.

May the eternal light give, not a reason for living and working, but a sense of completeness which makes the search for any such reason unnecessary.

Failing that, the only incentives are fear and gain—fear, which implies the oppression of the people; gain, which implies the corruption of the people.

Manual labour. Time entering into the body. Through work man turns himself into matter, as Christ does through the Eucharist. Work is like a death.

We have to pass through death. We have to be killed—to endure the weight of the world. When the universe is weighing upon the back of a human creature, what is there to be surprised at if it hurts him?

Work is like a death if it is without an incentive. We have to act, renouncing the fruits of action.

To work—if we are worn out it means that we are becoming submissive to time as matter is. Thought is forced to pass from one instant to the next without laying hold of the past or the future. That is what it means to obey.

Joys parallel to fatigue: tangible joys, eating, resting, the pleasures of Sunday . . . but not money.

No poetry concerning the people is authentic if fatigue does not figure in it, and the hunger and thirst which come from fatigue.

POSTSCRIPT, FIFTY YEARS LATER[1]

What could I add to these lines, written nearly half a century ago? Light for the spirit and nourishment for the soul, Simone Weil's work does not have to be brought 'up to date,' since it emanates from that summit of being which overhangs all times and places. How could one put a date on a particular thought by Plato or Marcus Aurelius, a verse by Aeschylus, or the utterance of a Shakespearean hero ? The same is true, and in exemplary fashion, for Simone Weil. True light does not fade, and a true fountain need never be replenished.

To speak of what is timeless is also to speak of what is universal. The undeserved privilege of presenting Simone Weil's first book to the public has brought me countless favourable comments from the four corners of the globe. What strikes me most about these is that they come from individuals of such diverse backgrounds, social status, cultural milieu, etc, and that

[1] Thibon's postscript in Simone Weil, *La Pesanteur et la grâce* (Paris: Plon, 1991) translated by Mario von der Ruhr.

reading this work has left a deep impression on all their souls, as they found in it the revelation of an inner truth for which they had, up until then, been waiting in vain.

At the twilight of a century whose accelerated history has led to the rise and fall of so many idols, this book increasingly appears like a message from eternity, addressed to eternal man, this 'Nothingness capable of God,' who is enslaved by gravity and liberated by grace.

GUSTAVE THIBON
DECEMBER 1990